Catherine L. Scott

ACCENT BOOKS
Denver, Colorado

Unless otherwise noted, all Scripture references are quoted from the King James Version of the Bible.

ACCENT BOOKS

A division of Accent Publications, Inc.
12100 West Sixth Avenue
P.O. Box 15337
Denver, Colorado 80215

Library of Congress Catalog Card Number 86-73187

ISBN 0-89636-237-X

This book is dedicated to my mother,
Rae Leona Bushey
who always thought I could . . . .
I miss her loving presence every day.

In Appreciation

There are many people who helped me in the writing of this book. The Lord graciously surrounded me with people whose talents and gifts supported and encouraged my explorations of this subject. I will thank a few of them here, and give thankful praise to God for them all.

To my husband, Tom, our daughter, Brandie and son, Jeff, who grow with me and teach me so well.

To my sister, Dorothy, who loved me as an often bratty child, and loves me as a sometimes bratty adult; to my sister Mary, who has survived and shared her own walk through the valley.

To Debbie Pruett, who so lovingly shares and comforts; to Elaine Hooper, who daily eases the burdens; to Judy Laughlin, Jessica Loeper, Cindy Balsam and Jewell Taylor, who help me to explore with my heart and my mind. You prayed, edited, laughed, listened and hoped with me.

To the service users, directors, staff, and volunteers of the Self-Help Center, who shared with and patiently taught me.

Thank you for being a part of my life.

Contents

Introduction   7

Chapter

  1 Your Home—Zoned For Abuse   11

  2 Target Zone—Physical Abuse   15

  3 Target Zone—Emotional Abuse   28

  4 Target Zone—Spiritual Abuse   41

  5 Exploring Your Emotions   49

  6 Scriptural Realignment   66

  7 Misplaced Manhood: The Battering
    Husband   81

  8 Childhood of Fear: The Effects of Violent
    Behavior In Your Home   102

  9 Your Alternatives   114

 10 Information For The Woman Who
    Separates   134

 11 Choosing a Counselor   151

 12 The Narrow Path   161

A Special Note to the Reader   165

Resources   167

Bibliography   183

Introduction

"So that we may boldly say, The Lord is my helper, and I will not fear what man shall do unto me." (Hebrews 13:6)

Violence in today's family strikes with devastating force, leaving in its wake women who are confused, ashamed and alone, children who may be doomed to repeat the cycles of violence, and men whose lives are a tangled web of frustration and aggression.

As a volunteer advocate in a secular domestic violence/ sexual assault program, I have provided crisis intervention, support and information to men and women whose lives are affected by violent behavior. Their heart-wrenching stories of degradation, fear and turmoil, and their confusion as to the causes and effects of violent behavior, have forced me to re-examine my own attitudes about abuse. I have taught and so learned; reached out and so been touched; comforted, and so been comforted.

There are many excellent books which provide insight into domestic violence, books which have been carefully researched and have solid documentation and valuable statistics. I am grateful to those authors for providing the background information necessary for me to undertake this book. But, in the course of my training and work as an advocate, and in further researching family violence, I found that few writers have approached in depth the issues of specific concern to the Christian woman who is a victim of spouse abuse, the issues which comprise the core of her faith. Christian writers have published hundreds of books which focus on marriage or family life, but I have not read one which specifically deals with the realities of violence in the Christian home.

Lovestruck is written for the Christian woman who is living or has lived in an abusive relationship. The men and women with whom I have worked as an advocate spoke with me in strict confidentiality, and I have not betrayed that trust here. None of the examples I give are direct quotes from one person, nor have I chosen to focus on one "real life" story. I have, instead, written of common experiences and feelings in abusive relationships. By recognizing and defining the abuse in your home, you will be better prepared to use the worksheets and suggestions provided to help you plan to escape the abuse you now suffer.

If you have sought help from a secular counselor well-versed in domestic violence, you may be struggling to balance your belief in God with concepts based on secular psychology or sociology. If you have chosen to approach your pastor about abusive behavior in your family, you may have encountered an inability to empathize with the many effects domestic violence has on its victims. Like thousands of women, you may have kept silent, hidden the bruises, and denied yourself needed assistance.

In reading this book, you may be able to pinpoint some elements of abuse in your relationship. Some examples given will coincide with your experiences, some will not. Defining the abuse as physical, psychological or spiritual may help you to understand how you are vulnerable, but you will find that most abusive behavior touches all three areas. Instead of puzzling over which "category" you should assign to the abuse in your relationship, simply recognize its existence, move on to explore your feelings, and utilize your abilities to choose alternatives to remaining a victim of abuse.

Information about domestic violence isn't enough. It does not address the Christian woman's spiritual needs. Careful application of Biblical principles to family problems often opens a clear path to safety. God is the only final authority on any subject, and so it must be here.

I have tried to provide hope, Biblical foundations and concrete guidelines. This book may not contain definitive answers to any or all of your questions about domestic violence, nor will it produce magical solutions to your current problems. If it helps you to explore your feelings, sheds light during a time of darkness, and/or strengthens your resolve toward positive change, it will have served its purpose. As with any book other than the Bible, there is both wheat and chaff between these pages. Sift them carefully; give yourself time to absorb the information as it applies to your situation. Time spent in prayer and Bible study will lead you far beyond any counsel this book may contain. Take what you need from here and leave the rest.

Chapter 1
Your Home—Zoned For Abuse

"Plead my cause, O Lord, with them that strive with me: fight against them that fight against me." (Psalm 35:1)

A woman involved in an abusive relationship lives in a war zone. The war may be undeclared, but is never cold. Her marriage is the battleground, she and her spouse the combatants, their children the ravaged civilians. Unchecked, abusive behavior will escalate and, predictably, become more frequent.

Society is inundated by violent behavior. Television, movies, books and the news media provide us with a never-ending flood of violence-oriented material, and we absorb it willingly. What constitutes violent or abusive behavior? How you answer that question may help you to understand how abuse affects you personally, and to identify your "target zones."

In later chapters, we will explore the profile of the man who batters, the effects of violence on children and some alternatives to remaining in a violent relationship. This chapter, and those immediately following, will explain the cycles of abuse, help define abusive behavior, and explore some effects a victim of domestic violence may experience.

The Cycle of Abuse

In her book, *The Battered Woman,* Lenore E. Walker defines and explains her research which indicates that incidents of violent behavior in a family are cyclic in nature.¹ These occurrences take place over and over in three distinct phases: the *Tension-Building Phase,* the *Acute Battering Incident,* and *Kindness and Contrite, Loving Behavior.* Recognizing and understanding each phase may help you to identify the cycles of abuse in your own relationship.

The Tension-Building Phase

Many victims of abuse identify this stage as the one in which she "walks on eggshells" in her home. The man who batters her may be irritable, critical of everyone around him, or verbally abusive to her and the children. If he drinks, he may increase his consumption of alcohol. His wife avoids upsetting him, stays out of his way, or tries to comply with all his demands. He may provoke arguments in which he pushes, shoves or slaps her, but he is not yet out of control. If a woman has lived in this kind of relationship long enough to have seen the cycle before, she knows that he will eventually erupt into further violence, but she has no way of knowing what will trigger it.

The Acute Battering Incident

This is the shortest phase, usually lasting from a few minutes to twenty-four hours. During this time, the batterer rages out of control, his actions triggered by a casual comment or minor disagreement. Like a nuclear reactor which suddenly reaches critical mass, the abusive man reacts to his own inner turmoil with unbridled destruction. He may waken his spouse from sleep to beat her, intent upon "teaching her a lesson." It is in this phase that law enforcement may be called. Whether drunk, under the influence of drugs, or sober, the batterer may seriously injure his wife, while continuing to administer "punishment." If he is not stopped, he may kill her.

Kindness and Contrite, Loving Behavior

The battered woman may be convinced that the man she sees during this phase is her husband in his "true" form. He is kind and solicitous. He may be truly sorry that he was "forced" to discipline her during phase two. He may buy her gifts and shower her with attention. Ignoring her injuries, the woman may be convinced that the abuse will never reoccur. This phase generally lasts a shorter time than stage one, but much longer than stage two, depending upon how quickly the man begins to give in to pressure and frustration. Eventually he begins phase one again as his tension builds and the entire cycle repeats itself.

Because these cycles can span several months, it may be difficult to recognize their progress in your relationship. Remember the acute battering incident and review the emotional climate in your home in the days preceding it. You will most likely be able to identify a period during which he became increasingly tense. Try to determine if the explosion into violence was followed by a period of calmness or loving attention.

Identify, if you can, the phase currently being played out in your home. Carefully examine the last few days with your spouse in order to determine if he is beginning to become nervous or agitated again. The line between phase three and phase one may be fuzzy, but preparing yourself for increased tension and possible abusive behavior may keep you from being caught unaware in the cycle.

Hopefully these explanations of the phases in the cycle of violence may also help you to step back and observe some of the realities about the violent behavior in your family.

The focus now turns to you: how violent behavior affects you, your feelings, your relationship to God, and how you perceive yourself. Many women find it difficult to set aside their concern and responsibility for others and to look within themselves. Christian women, particularly, are oriented toward service to others. But, if you are a victim of domestic violence, your body, mind and spirit have been under attack. You need to assess the damage, and be prepared to make decisions. Job 11:18 says, "And thou shalt be secure, because there is hope; yea, thou shalt dig about thee, and thou shalt take thy rest in safety."

13

While "digging about," seek to grasp a balanced perspective of who and what you are. A prayerful look inward allows God to reveal His plans for you. Your true strengths and weaknesses can be more easily discerned. As you begin to honestly review your past experiences with the aid of God's Word, you can look to the future secure in His will, full of hope, with a clearer view of yourself. *In almost every instance of physical abuse, the husband has set you up through psychological or emotional abuse to feel as if you deserve the physical abuse.* That is why this deeper, clearer look inside, filtered through prayer and the Bible, is essential to your concept of yourself.

You reflect the image of God. Abusive behavior in your family affects you physically, emotionally, and spiritually. We will look at each of these areas separately, then as a whole, in order to fully explore the impact of domestic violence on your life.

FOOTNOTES

[1] "Cycle of Violence Theory" from *The Battered Woman* by Lenore Walker. Copyright © 1979 by Lenore E. Walker. Reprinted by permission of Harper & Row, Publishers, Inc.

Chapter 2
Target Zone—Physical Abuse

"In thee, O Lord, do I put my trust: let me never be put to confusion. Deliver me in thy righteousness, and cause me to escape: incline thine ear unto me, and save me. Be thou my strong habitation, whereunto I may continually resort: thou hast given commandment to save me; for thou art my rock and my fortress. Deliver me, O my God, out of the hand of the wicked, out of the hand of the unrighteous and cruel man." (Psalm 71:1-4)

Physical violence is the most easily recognized form of abuse. Men and women in our society are quick to identify punching, kicking, biting or the use of weapons as violent behavior. Unfortunately, many perceive slapping, pushing, pinching or shaking someone with whom we are angry as non-abusive. But acts which cause little or no physical pain or leave no marks must also be considered abusive if they are used in anger to control someone else, or to release our own frustrations.

In the chapter on emotional battering, we will identify some abusive words and attitudes used by batterers to lower a woman's self-esteem and cause her to doubt her self-perceptions. Verbal abuse generates fear and confusion; emotional degradation can separate a woman from communication with God and with other people. She may be psychologically primed to accept physical violence as another way for her spouse to control and demean her. Her husband may encourage her to believe that she can never escape the abuse. As his need to batter escalates, he often uses his wife's vulnerability to his anger to justify becoming physically abusive.

If you are in a physically violent relationship, be careful not to minimize the effects of even minor "hands-on" treatment by your partner. To do so may be literally placing your life in jeopardy.

Doctors and nurses in emergency rooms and clinics see the awful results of family violence every day. Many women are hospitalized with broken bones, concussions, burns, cuts, or internal injuries. Others are treated for bruises, scrapes, black eyes, and released to return to the abusive relationship. A woman may deny that her husband beat her. She may admit that he caused her injuries, but feel that she deserved the abuse. Many others simply cover the bruises, stay home, or avoid friends and family until their bodies heal.

While you may not think you need to see a doctor if your injuries seem to be minor, there are two reasons why you should reconsider. Because the explosive violence is such a shock mentally and physically, women often do not realize how badly they are injured until hours or even days have passed. Bruises and soreness may not alarm you, but it is possible for internal injuries, concussions, sprains and other damage to occur even if the batterer used what appeared to be little force.

Dr. Joseph Primrose, Director of Emergency Medical Services at Wyoming Medical Center advises, "Any patient who is experiencing pain caused by her injuries should contact a doctor in order to insure that no serious damage has resulted. Bruises, cuts, or abrasions can be observed and recorded. The doctor should be made aware that the patient's injuries are the result of her husband's actions. If, at that time or in the future, the patient chooses to file assault charges or needs to obtain a restraining order against the batterer, she will be able to obtain this record from her doctor or hospital as legal documentation of injuries. This record lends support to a woman's claim that her husband has been violent. Police and judges are often more willing to accept a woman's complaint when it is possible to show that the spouse has a history of abusive behavior."

The cycle of abuse may be played out again and again, and each incident increases the woman's chances of being seriously harmed. Because her self-esteem is further damaged by each period of psychological abuse, the woman becomes progressively less capable of discerning what constitutes normal marital conflict, less aware of the horror of the abuse. Her isolation from others can prevent her from sharing her alarm at the level of abuse in her relationship as can mistaken loyalty.

According to statistics compiled by the National Coalition Against Domestic Violence, one-third of all men who beat their wives also beat their children. Pregnancy, with its related emotional and financial stress, often triggers physical violence, possibly causing a miscarriage. Physical or mental handicaps in newborns are also sometimes attributable to the mother having been severely beaten.

Studies have shown that alcohol is a factor in as many as 80% of incidents in which domestic violence occurs.[1] In the past, it was assumed that the batterer lost control because he was drinking and was more likely to become violent. New data indicates that drinking is not the cause of the battering incident. Instead, it is now thought that men who batter drink in order to have an excuse to beat their wives. In phase three the wife will often be told by her husband that he does not remember the acute battering incident, and find that he accepts little personal responsibility for his loss of control. He may placate his spouse with promises to stop drinking, convincing her that the abuse occurs only because he drinks too much. In all likelihood, though, even if the batterer quits drinking, he will continue to follow the cycle of abusive behavior. Alcohol abuse, and any other form of substance abuse, may be related to the battering only in that it gives the husband an excuse to become violent and avoid the consequences of his behavior.

Sexual abuse in marriage is often an adjunct to other physical violence. Some batterers force their wives into sexual acts as a part of the second phase of the cycle. Some men find violence itself to be sexually stimulating and are likely to display violence during intercourse whether or not they are being otherwise physically abusive at the time. As with all abusive behavior, sexual abuse is an attempt on the part of the batterer to control his spouse, and it has little to do with normal sexual desires. In extreme cases, wives have been forced to perform repulsive or degrading sexual acts, forced to have sex with other people or to watch others perform, and been violated by their husbands' use of objects for penetration. I know several women who have had hysterectomies or other serious gynecological procedures as a result of damage caused by their husbands' brutal actions. While the physical effects of sexual abuse can be horrifying, the emotional pain of such degradation leaves deeper scars.

Sometimes a wife initiates intercourse during phase one in order to relieve tension, hoping to delay or avoid her husband's violent outbursts. In phase two, she may submit to painful or humiliating acts, unable to overcome her husband's physical superiority, or may remain passive in hopes that, after his orgasm, her spouse will stop beating her. And, during phase three, she may overlook further roughness because he seems so sincerely repentant.

It is important to realize that a man who physically abuses his partner at any point in their relationship, before or after marriage, will probably continue in this behavior. If abuse has occurred more than once, it will most likely happen again. This violence almost always escalates. That is, pushing or slapping will eventually progress to more severe abuse if the batterer does not admit that he is using his physical strength as a way to control his wife and to release frustration. Without acknowledging his need for help to change his abusive behavior, he will repeat the cycle over and over. It is entirely possible that as these episodes occur with more frequency and/or violence, they may result in the woman being killed.

Whether or not this book helps in any other way, there is one critical overwhelming truth every wife needs to etch in the very fabric of her heart and being: *No one deserves to be beaten.* Nothing you have done or said, no error you have made, no sins you may have committed give your partner the right to punish you. If you have been physically abused by your spouse, you have a right to remove yourself from that danger and to seek help. He is responsible for his own actions.

It is *not* safe to assume that your spouse will realize the extent of his problem. Christian or not, he may not be convinced that his actions are wrong. Even if he recognizes the problem, he may not be able to stop his abusive behavior without professional help. Consider what may happen the next time abuse occurs, and make plans now to protect yourself and your children. Carefully examine the circumstances which preceded the most recent episode of abuse. The more information you gather concerning your situation, the more able you are to make rational decisions. Pay attention to the patterns of his abusive behavior. If he chooses not to exert self-control or to seek help in changing his behavior, you must determine how best to protect yourself and your children.

The police may be called by a victim, the children, or neighbors when a dispute erupts into violence. Though much has changed with the advent of increased knowledge and understanding of what happens in a violent home, you may still be faced with unfair and even dangerous attitudes toward domestic violence when seeking help from law enforcement. Many women have called the police during a domestic assault only to have the officers virtually ignore their injuries if they are not life-threatening. They sometimes advise both partners to "kiss and make up," as if nothing more than a minor disagreement had taken place!

Remain as calm as possible when talking to the police. Tell them exactly what has occurred, detailing any injuries you may have sustained. If your husband blames you for starting the fight, or tells the police you are lying about what happened, simply restate the facts. Do not argue with your husband. Direct all your comments to the officers. You may also want to speak to the police in another room, away from your husband.

You can request that the officers make a report, and that you be given the number of the report in case you need it later. If you want to have your husband arrested, the police can remove him from your home. If you are willing to press assault charges, it may force your husband to accept responsibility for his violent behavior. However, it is still a reality that most judges will not force a batterer to obtain counseling, even if they are aware of repeated offenses. And, in addition to the emotional turmoil, having your husband arrested may result in a loss of income for the family. Lawyers and court fees are a drain on a family's finances. You must carefully weigh your situation and decide if legal intervention is the most effective way to escape your husband's abuse.

If you believe that your husband may become violent again, you may want to leave for awhile. Ask the officer to wait until you gather a few things, and to insure that your husband does not follow you. If you show the officer that you are concerned about your own safety, and about protecting your children, it is more likely that he will take you seriously.

If, like some batterers, your spouse is able to display a calm and slightly bewildered expression when confronted about his behavior, the police may not believe that he actually assaulted you. If they ignore what you tell them, restate your concerns, but be aware that you may have to rely on your own plan of action to take you and your children to a safe place.

Remember, if your spouse was raised in a violent home, was physically abused, or saw his mother beaten, he may think that his violent actions are normal. He may believe that he has the right, as your husband, to control you and his children with violent behavior.

Before the tension in your home erupts into violence again, call your local police and ask them what their policies are concerning domestic violence calls. Find out what you can expect from them should you call for help. If the police are sensitive to the issues of domestic violence, they will inform your husband that a physical assault on any person is a criminal offense. They may urge your husband to leave, or may offer to take you to a safe place.

We will discuss other steps you can take to protect yourself in the chapter on alternatives. If, however, you believe that it is likely that severe abuse will take place soon, act now to protect yourself and your children. You do not need to take any permanent steps yet, but if you are in danger, do not hesitate to plan for a safe escape.

Common Questions About Physical Abuse

Q. My husband frequently becomes very angry and sometimes shakes or pushes me. Should I consider leaving him even though he has never really hurt me?

A. Perhaps the abusive behavior in your home is not as severe as some of the examples presented. *The urgency expressed in this chapter is directed toward the woman who believes she is in imminent danger of being physically abused, one whose husband has shown himself to be violent and seems likely to injure her in the near future.* Complete the worksheets at the end of each chapter. These will help you to detail the abuse you have experienced. You alone are in the best position to assess how safe you and your children are.

If the abuse is currently mild and infrequent, you may choose to remain in your home and begin to seek help from a pastor, domestic violence organization, or friends. Remember that physical violence almost always becomes more frequent and severe. Ignoring the problem will not make it go away. Learn more about domestic violence, study its causes and effects. Through prayer, study of the Scriptures, counseling, and realization of your God-given self-worth, begin to make reasonable and safe choices in your life.

Q. I have no money, no job, and no transportation. How can I leave?

A. If you feel that an abusive episode will happen again, try to save some money each week or month from your household budget and keep it hidden in case you need it. If you have confided in a friend that abuse is taking place in your family, you may be able to ask this friend for a loan, or to give you a ride to a safe place. Explore some possibilities. Leaving home without clothes, money or a car is very difficult, but it is not impossible. Your safety and that of your children must be your first priority.

When making a plan of action, call legal aid, your local domestic violence agency, or a lawyer to be sure you are acting in accord with the law should you leave and take your children. If you ask a friend for help, be certain that you will not be endangering her legally or putting her at risk from the batterer. In a small number of states, anyone who helps remove children from joint custody with their father could be charged with aiding and abetting. Your local police, a lawyer, legal aid, or local domestic violence agency should be able to give you guidelines concerning these questions. Ask about family violence protection orders or restraining orders which are issued by the court to keep the batterer away from the spouse. Consider filing temporary child custody requests if you decide to leave. Complete the plan of action chart at the end of chapter nine, and resolve to use the plan if you believe you are in danger.

Q. My husband often breaks things in the house, and once destroyed a fish tank I had. He has never hit me or the children, but I am afraid that he might.

A. Many abusive men turn their anger on objects as well as people. They may destroy anything within reach, but often manage to avoid damaging their own personal possessions, focusing instead on things belonging to their wives or children. Some will brutally kill a family pet if his wife is especially fond of it. You should be aware that this behavior can also escalate to include you and/or your children. Make plans as suggested in the chapter on alternatives just as if he had already assaulted you.

Q. I hit my husband during our last argument. Doesn't that make me as guilty as he is, even if he hit me first?

A. Let me repeat what I said before. *No one deserves to be beaten.* You are not alone. Many women do strike back in anger and fear. You may have made a conscious decision to fight back, or simply reacted, attempting to protect yourself or a child by defensive behavior. Even if you struck the first blow, you need to accept that you, too, are capable of violent behavior and that other alternatives are available to both men and women. Read the chapter on Scriptural Realignment and learn to judge your own responsibilities.

Q. My husband says he will kill himself if I leave. How can I take that chance?

A. Many men threaten suicide as a way of manipulating their wives. In the chapter dealing with the batterer, you will read some of the reasons for these threats. Any threat of suicide must be taken seriously, and the possibility that someone you love may harm himself is frightening. While you must accept that he may indeed attempt suicide should you leave, think about the fact that he may seriously injure or kill you or your children if you stay.

Choose a moment when you can discuss with your husband why he would choose self-destruction rather than seek counseling. Be very careful when confronting him, and do not continue with the discussion if he becomes threatening or abusive. If he remains calm, explain to him that you are concerned that he will harm himself. Assure him that you love him. Tell him that you want to remain in the home, but that his behavior makes that dangerous to you and/or your children. Offer to help him find a counselor who can help him explore both his anger and his thoughts of suicide.

However, do not allow him to use suicide threats to force you into remaining in a dangerous situation. Make it clear that the violence in your home destroys the love and companionship which God intended for marriage. It slowly kills self-esteem, mutual sharing, and trust within the family. But remember that you cannot jeopardize your safety because your spouse refuses to seek help.

If you must leave suddenly, or if your husband refuses to listen to your suggestions, consider contacting a friend, pastor, or law enforcement officer to check on your husband and help him to deal with your absence. Write him a letter which explains that it is impossible for you to live with the abuse and why, from a Biblical as well as practical perspective. This may be the evidence he needs to change his abusive behavior.

Q. My husband refuses to allow me to see a doctor when I'm sick or to have check-ups for the children. Does he have the right to do this?

A. Refusing to allow you to obtain such care is abusive behavior. Your husband may be worried about the financial strain of medical bills. Decide together how to re-adjust your budget to cover such costs, or arrange to make payments to a doctor with whom you have discussed your financial difficulties.

I am a firm believer in God's awesome power to heal. But a Christian man who refuses his spouse or children the opportunity to seek conventional medical care because he insists that all healing must come miraculously from God is being abusive. You have a right to competent medical care in addition to your faith, and you have an obligation to provide reasonable care for your children. If you can work out an agreement with your husband concerning medical care, do so. If no compromise is possible, seek additional help or counsel from an authority your husband respects.

Q. I believe that God will protect me and heal my marriage. Doesn't God have the power to change our lives?

A. Yes. He does. God can and does work in all areas of our lives. I believe in His saving grace, His unconditional love for us, and that He will never forsake His children. The Psalms frequently point out God's protective presence in eloquent praise: *"The Lord is my strength and my shield; my heart trusted in him, and I am helped: therefore my heart greatly rejoiceth; and with my song will I praise him" (Psalm 28:7).*

God is never limited in the ways He provides help for us. Capable of awesome miracles, He sometimes uses ordinary means to meet our needs. And even though a mundane solution to problems may be at hand, He sometimes chooses to reveal His power in dramatic fashion.

In all of Christ's miracles, we see His unerring knowledge of what is needed to accomplish His perfect purpose, and His ability to engender hope and gratitude where there was once only guilt and condemnation.

The means by which God offers protection and healing will be different for each woman reading this book. God may miraculously heal your body, mind and spirit, and convict your husband of his wrongdoing. He may provide a minister who is knowledgeable about the cause and effects of violence to help your husband change his abusive behavior. You may find support through a secular organization concerned with family violence and be helped through Bible study as to what choices are yours to make. Second Timothy 1:7 promises you: "For God hath not given us the spirit of fear; but of power, and of love, and of a sound mind." You may face difficult, traumatic choices, but as you seek His will, God will give you wisdom and a sound mind to make those decisions.

FOOTNOTES

[1] Statistics obtained from the National Coalition Against Domestic Violence.

Has There Been Abuse?

Use these pages to record any form of physical violence you may have endured. By making a list of such abuse, you will be able to more honestly face the seriousness of your situation. In chapter five, you can refer to this list while exploring your emotions. In chapter nine, this list will help you form your plan of action. Use it when you pray for yourself, your children, and your spouse.

Physical Abuse

Has your husband ever:

_____ pushed you

_____ used force to keep you from leaving or seeking help

_____ thrown objects at you

_____ slapped you

_____ thrown you to the ground

_____ grabbed you by the hair

_____ choked you

_____ punched you

_____ bit you

_____ kicked you

_____ burned you

_____ refused to allow you to obtain medical attention when you were sick or injured

_____ locked you out of the house

_____ locked you in a room

_____ raped or otherwise sexually abused you

_____ used weapons (including guns, knives, sticks, lamps, belts, etc.) to harm you

_____ other

Has this physical abuse resulted in:
_____ bruises
_____ cuts
_____ scrapes
_____ broken bones
_____ cracked bones, ligament or tendon damage
_____ black eyes
_____ dislocations or sprains
_____ complications caused by a lack of proper medical attention
_____ concussions
_____ broken teeth
_____ nerve damage
_____ aches or soreness
_____ double vision or blurred vision
_____ difficulty breathing
_____ miscarriage
_____ mental or physical damage to an unborn child
_____ gynecological (female) difficulties
_____ other

This is by no means a complete list. However, it may help you to recall some assaults you may have ignored. Later, we will explore the emotional damage that can occur as a result of physical brutality.

But whether or not you have experienced any physical abuse, emotional abuse may have taken place. We will explore the effects of emotional abuse in the next chapter.

27

Chapter 3
Target Zone—Emotional Abuse

"There is that speaketh like the piercings of a sword: but the tongue of the wise is health." (Proverbs 12:18)

Emotional abuse always occurs when physical abuse takes place. One cannot be hurt physically without perceiving that hurt on an emotional level as well. A woman who is pushed to the ground by an unknown purse-snatcher may be bruised or scraped, but she will also feel angry, frightened, resentful, sad, or any combination of these emotions. How much more, then, must a woman who is physically assaulted by someone she knows, loves or trusts be emotionally affected? A man who uses his superior strength to batter injures you physically. Emotionally, he attempts to exert a control over you which should not be in his hands.

However, it is also true that emotional abuse can occur without physical abuse. Though less obvious than bodily assault, such abuse is as damaging as physical violence. Verbal assaults wound the mind and emotions just as physical blows wound the body. Hurtful words and attitudes leave wounds which often heal more slowly than physical scars.

Words used by a husband to control his wife and, often, their children are emotional abuse. This abuse "brainwashes" its victims. For instance, by constant verbal repetition, the batterer can convince his wife that his viewpoints and perceptions are always correct, never to be questioned. Even if he has never attacked her physically, she may be frightened that he would if she confronted him about the emotional effect of his words on her. She begins to believe that she is disobedient to his leadership, and because she is unable to meet his strict standards, she deserves his angry tirades. He may also display attitudes which demean women, and which indicate that he believes his wife is inferior. Often, a wife will become convinced that her husband is invincible, and she is worthless. She becomes more of a slave to his anger, afraid to even think of escaping his abuse.

Batterers typically display extreme possessiveness and jealousy. These attitudes reflect his belief that his wife is a possession, something he owns and over which he must maintain control. In extreme cases, he may demand that she remain at home, totally isolated from friends, neighbors and family members. He may actually lock her in the house and disconnect the phone to insure her imprisonment. In his jealousy, he imagines that she is constantly unfaithful to him, or would be if he did not watch her so carefully. It is common for an abusive husband to insist that his wife dress in sexy or revealing clothes in which she is uncomfortable, and then become infuriated if other men pay attention to her. Though he may repeatedly tell his spouse how worthless (or unattractive, stupid, lazy, etc.) she is, he may threaten to kill her if she even speaks to another man.

This type of confusion as to the true intent of the batterer's words is common. Many victims of verbal abuse are receiving and trying to understand some very mixed-up signals from their spouses. On one hand, he degrades her verbally and may tell her that she brings on the physical abuse because she is a "rotten wife." On the other hand, he is willing to go to almost any lengths to insure that no one threatens his place as the focus of her life. This may include friends, neighbors, children and other family members and, most certainly, other men.

Many women ask, "If I'm such a terrible person, why is he so afraid someone else will want me?"

Though the abusive man may be insanely jealous of his wife, he may engage in several sexual affairs. He often flaunts these infidelities, rationalizing that having a "frigid" wife forced him to seek extramarital sex, and insists upon relating the details of his affair to his wife. Or, he may refuse to talk to her when confronted with her anger over a known affair, telling her that it is none of her business and beating her if she continues to confront him. Any of these tactics can cause a wife to be caught up in a whirlwind of emotional reactions which include guilt, fear, betrayal, and anger. The woman may believe she must accept the responsibility for her husband's actions, thinking that she drove him to adultery.

If the abuse in your own relationship is not yet as blatant as these examples, name-calling and other verbal attacks on your character, physical appearance, attitudes or abilities may be present. The man who calls you dirty names characterizes you as less than human or labels you immoral. The man who constantly belittles you by using terms such as ugly, fat, lazy, or stupid strikes deeply and subtly at your self-image. In submitting to this abuse, you run the risk that this constant verbal barrage will damage your self-esteem and that you will begin to believe that his labels really reflect who you are. Ignoring his remarks is a short-term defense because they reach deep within you at an emotional level.

Alone or coupled with physical abuse, verbal attacks can have devastating effects. Instead of clear, honest emotions through which God can work, you may develop a tangled web of confused feelings. You may no longer perceive God's guidance for your life or your worth in His eyes. You may be too overwhelmed by the hurt caused by verbal abuse. Constant criticism slowly chips away your confidence in your abilities. "Nothing I do is ever right!" is a common statement from women in emotionally abusive relationships.

In your roles as wife, mother, career woman, or a combination of these roles, you may find that your husband seldom or never thinks you have done enough, or done it well enough. Be aware of what is happening and take stock of the damage this criticism does to you.

If you begin to mistrust your own perceptions, believing

yourself to be the sole cause of these attacks, or that the words are true, you may spend countless hours trying to change what your husband tells you is wrong with you. If you are constantly "on guard" when offering opinions, sharing ideas, casually conversing with your spouse, or find yourself fearful of his reaction to your conversations with other people, he has effectively limited your ability to communicate with others. Eventually, you may see yourself as unable to take charge of any situation or to protect yourself from the barrage of abuse.

Domestic violence occurs in cycles and your feelings may follow the phases. During the tension-building phase, you may feel anxious, nervous, "on edge." This is because you are walking in an emotional mine field. Any of the hidden explosives may be triggered, you fear, by a misstep on your part. In reality, nothing you do is actually the reason for your husband's abusive behavior and nothing you do can effectively restrain it.

Mounting verbal attacks, and your spouse's critical attitudes during phase one may create feelings that are hard for you to identify. If you can, begin to explore some of the emotions you feel during this tension-building phase. Can you identify what he says that makes you feel angry? How do you handle that anger? Do you hold it in, afraid that confronting him or snapping back will trigger another fight? Do you lash out at your children? Do you avoid other people? Women in abusive relationships sometimes isolate themselves from others because they are embarrassed by what is happening in their families. If you feel lonely, check to see if your life has become devoid of friends and family with whom you can share. Disappointment that your marriage is in trouble, guilt over raising your children in a violent home, and shame for the things you think you have done wrong are common feelings.

The episodes of violence may leave you with a feeling of unreality. You may feel as if you are in a nightmare. You may feel empty or enraged, or even wish that he would kill you so that you could be free from the ordeal. Resentment, confusion, desire for revenge may whirl inside you. Shock may keep you from thinking clearly and delay you from seeking help for your injuries.

As your husband moves into phase three, you may be distrustful of his attention to you. Or, relieved that he seems to understand how badly he hurt you, you might be happy that he cares so much. Feeling bitter, ashamed or betrayed is common. Yet, you may want to protect him or feel sorry for him.

Some women who experience the emotional upheavals common to abusive relationships become severely depressed. Constant fatigue, loss of appetite (or the desire to overeat), becoming less interested in activities you once enjoyed, and decreased interest in sex are all common symptoms of depression. If you suspect depression is a problem for you, contact your doctor. Often, there can be medical as well as emotional reasons for depression.

In the chapter on physical violence, we touched on the problem of sexual abuse in marriage. This affects deeply your emotional well-being and is a serious part of emotional abuse.

Sexual abuse is any coercion which forces you into an act to which you do not freely consent. In the chapter on Scriptural Realignment, we will explore what the Bible says about a wife's submission to her husband. A forced sexual act is not Biblical, and most states consider it rape even within marriage. Marital rape does not resemble making love with your husband as an act of sharing and pleasure. If you are hurt or feel degraded by what he demands from you, you are likely to feel angry and used by him. If your husband wants sex at inopportune times and places, or demands relations so frequently that it seems as though he is never satisfied, you may be confused as to whether you can and should ever refuse him. You may resent your husband's demands if he seldom tries to anticipate your desires or refuses to accept no for an answer. Perhaps the nature of his assaults is strictly verbal, but he makes clear what he considers to be your sexual inadequacies. He may label you "frigid" and continually threaten to seek other women.

It is possible that your husband may become furious if you try to initiate sex or if you propose a change in some aspect of lovemaking, accusing you of having had other sex partners. He may withhold sex as a means of punishing you for real or imagined wrongdoing. If you can explore other abuse, both physical and emotional, in your relationship, you may discover that the sexually-oriented abuse is just one aspect, a reflection of other ills. It is difficult for women to separate their sexual feelings from resentment, hurt, anger or fear of their husband. Do not be manipulated by accusations that your sex drive is inadequate. Verbal, physical, and spiritual abuse builds emotional walls. Your husband's disregard for your feelings can limit the pleasure with which you accept his sexual attentions.

Another aspect of emotional abuse is isolation. It is a common effect of family violence. The victim becomes more and more withdrawn as the abuse in her home escalates. Fear of the reactions of friends, neighbors, and relatives as well as shame that she isn't keeping her family happy and safe may force her to avoid making friends and seeking their companionship. Often, an abusive spouse will arrange his wife's day in such a way as to leave her no time in which to make friends. He may insist that she take him to work, and meet him for any coffee or lunch breaks. He may call her several times a day in order to effectively limit her outside contacts.

Your spouse may seem reluctant to accept your ideas or suggestions when making family decisions or may seem disinterested in your personal activities or interests. If he is not abusive, but frequently withdraws into silence in front of the television rather than spending time with you, he may be emotionally neglectful rather than abusive. The difference between abuse and neglect usually becomes clear when the relationship is viewed as a whole. Most of us neglect the people we love for short periods of time when we are unusually stressed, depressed, or grieved. Such neglect is not designed to hurt the other person; it is simply a result of preoccupation with our own problems. The partner may seem distant, or may want more time alone. Unlike abusive spouses, though, partners who may occasionally be neglectful will probably have displayed the ability to communicate well, and the relationship has a foundation of mutual support and respect. If the neglect does not result in one partner fearing or being manipulated by the other, the problem can usually be resolved with patient attempts to help the neglectful partner recognize the cause of the desire to turn inward.

Some men are simply not demonstrative of their emotions. Many husbands rely on their hard work and dedication to the family to prove their love. A man may be embarrassed by or may disapprove of showing affection in public. If he seldom becomes angry, is patient, shows that he respects you as a person, and is kind and considerate in other areas, appreciate him in words and in actions. You can encourage him to explore and express his feelings more openly as you assure him of your love. Let him know how much you value his displays of affection. He would benefit from your prayers, too, and from affirmation of his verbal and physical expressions of love.

A man may refuse to pay attention to his children or make it clear that he considers the children to be your responsibility with little or no help from him. These attitudes are abusive because they refuse to acknowledge your personhood and allow no room for growth in your life, give no aid or support when you may need it badly, and eliminate the sharing of responsibilities.

Loving confrontation about the neglectful or abusive attitudes your husband harbors can be extremely productive. Choose a time when he is least likely to become angry, a time when he might listen carefully. Explain calmly that you feel restricted, resentful, neglected, or wounded by his attitudes or actions. Be specific about what is making you unhappy. If you have trouble talking to him openly, consider writing him a letter, asking him to read it before talking about the problem.

If he refuses to listen to your opinions on the subject, it indicates an unwillingness to compromise. If such is the case, you might decide to undertake whatever reasonable course of action you had planned to discuss with him. Take the new job, go back to school, enroll the children in an art class as if he had agreed to the plan. If he becomes angry, tell him that you wanted it to be a mutual decision, but he refused to discuss it. Be willing to consider reasonable compromises, but resolve not to be bullied by your husband.

However, never confront a man who might become physically violent, nor one who is likely to verbally abuse you if you begin a discussion. If he perceives your actions as a threat to his domination, you or the children could be injured. If he is that abusive, one option you might consider is separating from him until he becomes aware of how damaging his abuse is to the family. Another is seeking out a Christian counselor, for both of you ideally, or you alone if he refuses to go.

If you are the wife of an alcoholic, you may endure abusive neglect coupled with verbal, physical and/or spiritual abuse. Though there are many similarities in the lives of spouses of alcoholics and wives of batterers, you may be dealing with two different problems: his alcoholism and his abusive behavior. They are closely meshed, and have many of the same root causes. Stopping one may inhibit the other, but your spouse may continue to be violent even if he is able to stop drinking.

Whether it is safe for you to remain in your home or if you must leave in order to protect yourself and your children, consider counseling with a minister or other professional who is knowledgeable about alcoholism. You may wish to attend meetings of Al-Anon to help bring your life into balance. They have excellent programs for loved ones of alcoholics based on Al-Anon's belief that one must only take responsibility for his or her own actions.

In reading this chapter, simply try to define what kind of emotional abuse you may be experiencing and how the abuse affects you. If you can write one emotion that you feel now, or have felt, and examine what happened in your relationship to trigger that particular emotion, you have taken a step toward honestly assessing the emotional ties to abusive behavior. Try not to label any emotion you feel as good or bad; don't attempt to judge what you are feeling until you can read the chapter on spiritual realignment. For now, take the opportunity to be honest with yourself concerning the reality of your emotions and the effects of emotional abuse.

Questions Concerning Emotional Abuse

Q. If you identify excessive criticism and name-calling as emotional abuse, is there anyone who has not been a victim?

A. Probably not. From the time we are children, we endure emotional and sometimes physical abuse in many forms. The child who comes home crying because someone at school teased her about having red hair may feel embarrassed, angry, or fearful of being different from other children. Without help to maintain her self-esteem, continued abuse will probably cause some emotional problems for the child. A woman who lives with constant verbal abuse from her spouse must have a deep commitment to her relationship with him. He has much greater power to hurt her than does a stranger or a casual acquaintance. The closer the relationship between two people, the more deeply the knife of emotional abuse stabs. This woman is a victim of the man who promised to "love, honor and cherish" her, and she may spend the rest of her life living with this abuse if she does not take steps to change her situation.

Identifying one's own victimization by others is painful. It is easier, in the short term, to pretend that the words don't hurt us, that we can withstand the pressure of their abuse. It takes great faith to ask God to help you recall the hurts, and to determine how you have been hurt. But once you do, you can use Biblically sound guidelines to protect yourself from further damage. In the chapter on alternatives, consider carefully what course of action best suits your situation.

Q. My husband often makes fun of my driving, my book-keeping, my friends. Sometimes the things he says are funny, but often they hurt. Is that verbal abuse?

A. It is abusive if your husband is aware that he is hurting you and makes no attempt to change his behavior. You have a responsibility to say calmly, "I feel hurt when you make jokes about me. Please don't laugh at the things I try to do." If you see an honest attempt on his part not to ridicule your efforts, he is sensitive to your feelings and doesn't want to hurt you. Thank him for his support. If he continues to make fun of you, or if it becomes worse, it is definitely verbal abuse, and you should take steps to protect yourself.

Q. As a Christian, I think I should be able to rise above my husband's name-calling and criticism, but sometimes he says something that hurts me deeply. Should I pretend I don't hear him?

A. Again, calmly telling your spouse that something he has said hurt or offended you is always best if it is safe for you to do so. Depending upon how severe the abuse is in your family, choose a time when you are most likely to be able to talk to your husband honestly about how his words affect you. Rising above the abuse only works if you can disregard the malice he intends. Most women cannot tolerate repeated or constant doses of this type of venom without having severe reactions to it.

Q. I realize that I nag my husband and complain that he doesn't make enough money. Am I being abusive?

A. Repeated verbal harrassment and put-downs are indeed abusive behavior. Read the chapter on Scriptural Realignment and write down some ways you can avoid this type of abuse. There are ways to express your concerns or opinions without becoming abusive to your spouse. If we learn to communicate in love, we have taken another step toward the type of intimacy God intended us to share.

Q. My son is in trouble at school and church for calling other children names, as well as for some pushing and hitting. Why does he act this way?

A. Some children who see violence in their homes act out their aggressions on other children. Your son obviously knows that he can get attention by calling other children names. If he witnesses abusive behavior at home, it is very likely that he will be abusive to others. He must be told, and *shown* by you, that abusive behavior will not be tolerated because it is not a godly expression of feelings. Your own behavior should reflect your commitment to non-abusive behavior. One of the keys to discouraging abusive behavior is consistent, attentive discipline. The child must not be allowed to use verbal or physical violence in order to release his frustration or to get his own way. Instead, offer alternative behaviors which are acceptable. Encourage non-abusive verbalization of his feelings. Other suggestions for helping your children avoid destructive behavior are included in the chapter on children.

Use the following pages to list the emotional abuse which may have occurred in your relationship and some of the effects of that abuse. Keep this list and use it in conjunction with chapters five and eight.

Evaluation of Emotional Abuse

Has your husband repeatedly:
___ labeled you as stupid, immoral or lazy
___ criticized your efforts as a cook, homemaker, mother, etc.
___ called you frigid or criticized you as a sexual partner
___ accused you of having affairs
___ criticized your physical appearance
___ refused to allow you to participate in decisions involving the family
___ refused to take joint responsibilities for the children
___ refused to allow you to leave the house
___ refused to allow you to work outside the home
___ denied you any encouragement concerning your job, your education, or any project in which you are interested
                                                                  •

____ withheld sex in order to punish you
____ denied your right to reasonable control over money
____ threatened to harm you and/or the children if you try to leave him
____ threatened to commit suicide if you leave him
____ tried to keep you from seeing your family or friends
____ ignored you when you try to discuss problems or situations
____ told you about affairs or bragged about relationships with other women
____ manipulated you with anger in order to keep you submissive
____ manipulated you with lies or by avoiding issues
____ humiliated or embarrassed you in front of others or in private
____ caused you to lose a job or friendship because of his interference
____ called you filthy names
____ criticized your background, race, ethnic heritage
____ followed you or checked up on you
____ made demeaning "jokes," alone or in front of others, about your abilities, appearance, or other things which are important to you
____ indicated that he believes women are inferior to men
____ indicated that he thinks you are valuable only as a sexual partner, cook, or housekeeper, etc., not as a person
____ stated that he does not think you are as smart as he is
____ abused a pet because he was angry
____ other _____

Has a counselor, police officer, doctor or judge:
____ told you that you must like the abuse because you remain with your spouse
____ acted as if they don't believe what you say has happened in your family
____ laughed when you told them what your husband called you, or acted as if your physical injuries were not important

____ indicated that you are incapable of making appropriate decisions concerning your situation
____ other _____

Has the emotional abuse resulted in your becoming:
____ fearful of your husband's anger
____ worried that he might become physically violent
____ convinced that you can do nothing properly
____ resentful of his control over you
____ bitter that he continues to act abusively
____ sorrowful that your family is in turmoil
____ fearful for your children's emotional and physical safety
____ angry because he treats you so badly
____ hateful of him or of yourself
____ convinced that you are as bad, stupid, crazy, lazy, or helpless as he says you are
____ convinced you are not sexually appealing or functional
____ anxious over losing friends because of his actions
____ embarrassed by his abusive attitudes in public
____ isolated from other people
____ afraid to contradict him or to offer differing opinions
____ afraid he will become angry over even small mistakes
____ convinced that you cannot be trusted with money, the car, or to make decisions
____ afraid he will harm you if you try to leave
____ prone to headaches, ulcers, other illnesses
____ depressed by your circumstances
____ terrified that you can never escape his abuse
____ convinced that you deserve the abuse
____ convinced that you are a bad mother
____ afraid he will seriously injure or kill you
____ other _____

Chapter 4
Target Zone—Spiritual Abuse

"The spirit of man will sustain his infirmity; but a wounded spirit who can bear?" (Proverbs 18:14)

Your spiritual being affects and is affected by your physical and emotional being. As a human being, each of these interrelated parts works in a balance which defines who you are. A woman who is battered physically and/or emotionally may despair spiritually. She may relinquish the lifelines which nurture her bond with God: Bible study, church attendance, or fellowship with other Christians.

"I will praise thee; for I am fearfully and wonderfully made: marvellous are thy works; and that my soul knoweth right well" (Psalm 139:14).

Being "fearfully and wonderfully made," our spirits strive for communion with our Creator. Spiritual nourishment refreshes our bodies and clears our perceptions. But this type of seeking for God's will takes time, time that may not be available to you. If, in your relationship, such demands are made of you that you are unable to find even a short time each day to study God's Word, you are being starved spiritually.

A "wounded spirit" is one who thinks she has been forsaken by God. She is so hurt physically and emotionally that she feels unable to reach for, much less grasp, God's outstretched hand. Hopelessness is like quicksand; the more she struggles with it, the more rapidly it saps her strength. She can no longer remember that God is holding her, that He has never left her.

41

Both physical and emotional abuse can have spiritual consequences. A spouse can abuse you spiritually by denying you the opportunity to study God's Word or to be with other Christians, by belittling your faith, or by accusing you of not being a properly submissive wife. Ironically, the spiritual area may be the one a Christian man may attack most effectively. If your spouse uses the Bible as a weapon against you, he may tear you apart verse by verse to prove how little you know, or how you fall short of the Biblical standards of a virtuous wife. While most counselors would classify this solely as emotional abuse, the Bible indicates that words and actions which strike deeply into the heart of your faith in God constitute spiritual battering. See I Peter 3:7,12; Ephesians 4:29-32; James 1:19-26; Romans 14:12,19; Ephesians 4:14-24.

The disciples were mocked and ridiculed because of their faith. Paul said of the apostles: "We are troubled on every side, yet not distressed; we are perplexed, but not in despair; persecuted, but not forsaken; cast down, but not destroyed" (II Corinthians 4:8,9). Spiritual distress, despair, feelings of abandonment and helplessness, and the destruction of faith can result from prolonged, intense abuse. The effects of the spiritual abuse the disciples endured were made less damaging only because of the gift of the "spirit of faith" which grew by the power of the Holy Spirit in them in order to further the gospel (II Corinthians 4:13).

Scripture condemns using God's Word in ways which twist or distort the message. The man who uses Scripture to discourage and condemn another is himself guilty of sin. (See Romans 14:12,13; 8:1; 2:1-11.) We are to use the Word for enlightenment, to convict hearts of sin, and to reflect Christ's love (Romans 15:4). Proverbs 30:10 instructs, "Accuse not a servant unto his master, lest he curse thee, and thou be found guilty."

Attacks which lower your self-esteem can be considered spiritual abuse because one's concept of self goes beyond the mind and centers in the spirit. Even the Christian woman who values herself because, " . . . while we were yet sinners, Christ died for us," can lose sight of her worth as God's child when she endures repeated abuse (Romans 5:8).

In Psalm 109, David cries out, "For the mouth of the wicked and the mouth of the deceitful are opened against me: they have spoken against me with a lying tongue. They compassed me about also with words of hatred; and fought against me without a cause. For my love they are my adversaries: but I give myself unto prayer. And they have rewarded me evil for good, and hatred for my love . . . . I am poor and needy, and my heart is wounded within me" (verses 2-5, 22).

I have referred to women who live in abusive relationships as "victims." To some women, the word victim implies an inability to cope with or to change their circumstances. If, in the preceding chapters, you have been able to identify the abusive behavior in your relationships and some of its effects on you, the first step toward moving out of the role of victim has been taken. Exploring and understanding your feelings toward the person you are and your self-concept may provide you with new ways to assess your relationship.

We use many mirrors to reflect our limited perception of God. We see His image in nature: its beauty, its power, and its order reflect those images of the Creator. We raise our voices in songs which reflect His glory and give tribute to His saving grace. We see "through a glass darkly," but this limited reflection brings us assurance of His existence and His hand in our lives. And though we try, rarely do we shine enough light on our own mirror to allow us to see His image reflected there.

Self-esteem is a foundational concept in psychology which has, I believe, too often been twisted and misused. Self-esteem in a Christian is firmly rooted in the fact that each person is chosen to exist by God, and the knowledge that God doesn't make junk! He cares—deeply, intimately, personally. "But the very hairs of your head are all numbered." (Read Matthew 10:29-31.)

You were created with worth by the Father. He did not need to create you. He *chose* to do so. We, of all His creations, have the greatest potential to reflect His image. We were chosen by Him to be mirrors, and it is on this concept that we can base the importance of our self-esteem.

"For ye are bought with a price: therefore, glorify God in your body, and in your spirit, which are God's" (I Corinthians 6:20).

God feeds your spirit with His Word and constantly provides nourishment to stimulate growth and reflect repentance. How you feel about yourself can be an honest realization that comes from spiritual recognition of your own faults and assets. Recognizing a God-given talent, the woman with adequate self-esteem will thank God for His provision and use her talent as He gives her opportunity. When shown a fault or weakness in herself, she will be thankful for His honesty and use Scriptural principles to combat the problem. But neither talents nor sins are the whole of God's judgment for you. Rather, He probes your heart, your intentions, your reliance upon Him to give guidance concerning all aspects of your life (Hebrews 4:12,13).

If you live in an abusive relationship, however, your self-image may have become distorted. Though you may see a helpless, incompetent woman, it is a false image. It reflects your husband's angry defensiveness, not God's gentle love. You may have been harassed and blamed so often, you cannot accurately assess your own qualities.

If you have been beaten physically, it has been painfully clear that you are not in control of that situation. Emotional abuse may have increased your confusion and isolation. If you have suffered verbal abuse in which your partner demeaned your abilities, you may have questioned whether you are indeed immoral, unreasonable, or even stupid. Through spiritual abuse you are distanced from the heart-knowledge of the healing self-acceptance God would have you feel. The raging storm of abuse has eroded your perceptions of yourself. Find that part of you that reflects God's image and begin to reposition your mirror to reflect your true worth.

Acknowledge that your partner's abusive behavior stems from inadequacies and frustrations within him and that you need not accept his battering. Take steps now to begin to protect yourself physically, emotionally and, especially, spiritually. Your plan of action should include ways in which you can protect yourself in each of these areas. Written words often carry greater impact than fleeting, scattered thoughts. Work through the exercises at the end of each chapter carefully and prayerfully. This can be the first step toward your refusal to accept further abuse.

Look for the woman God loves so much! She is there, waiting to be recognized, and God's image can be seen in her.

Some Common Concerns About Spiritual Abuse

Q. Doesn't the Bible say that a woman is to submit to her husband?

A. It certainly does, and it says so much more in the chapters which contain those verses. The Bible clearly indicates that marriage is structured to mirror the relationship between Christ and His church (Ephesians 5:23-27). It is impossible to picture Christ violently battering His beloved. His anger is holy, his jealousy perfect. His commitment to His children shows His faithfulness, never selfish protection or gain. His desire is not to control His followers, but to have them give their compliance willingly and lovingly. He nourishes, cherishes, leads in wisdom, encourages growth, and comforts fear. Read the chapter on re-alignment if you feel obligated to endure abuse because of misconceptions on proper submission.

Q. My husband tore up my Bible and won't let me go to church. How can I keep my faith under this type of abuse?

A. I have talked to many women whose husbands become very violent when confronted with a woman's desire to grow spiritually. He may perceive your faith as a threat to his control over you. (As, indeed, it is.) Remember that you have a direct link to God through prayer, and that He does not depend exclusively on the Bible or a church to provide for your needs.

No matter what happens, God the Holy Spirit indwells you (Joshua 1:9; Psalm 37:25,28; I Corinthians 6:19,20; Hebrews 13:5).

Consider what alternatives you have to simply accepting his refusal to allow you to pursue spiritual growth. If your husband is physically violent, you must try to assess how dangerous he is. But, he may not be a physical batterer. Instead, he may use emotional and spiritual abuse, refusing to respect or recognize your need for Bible study and fellowship. You may be able to enlist your minister's help in confronting him. He needs to be told that no one has the right to restrict another person in making reasonable personal choices. Consider, too, God's commands and counsel in I Corinthians 7:10-16. Your attitude and approach to him may be the very thing God will use to convict and restore him to loving fellowship.

Do not deliberately provoke him with references to his disbelief, or flaunt your beliefs to anger him. You may feel that the Lord would have you refuse to neglect your need to exercise your faith. Your predetermined plan of action will help you to see what steps would be the wisest for your situation.

Refer to the chapter on alternatives to identify what rights you have in this area. Understand that your husband's anger stems, in part, from his fear that you are committed to something which he does not understand. Pray every day that he will be shown how important the reality of God is in his life as well as yours.

Spiritual Abuse

Has your husband:

____ repeatedly criticized your faith
____ refused to allow you to read the Bible
____ refused to allow you to go to church or Bible study
____ called you a "fanatic"
____ insulted or become angry at your Christian friends
____ insulted or become angry at your pastor
____ made "jokes" or demeaned your faith in private or in front of others (including your children)
____ refused to allow you to teach your children about God
____ destroyed your Bible, study materials, or texts
____ used the Bible as a weapon to demean you
____ used the Bible to justify his abusive behavior
____ indicated that you should submit to his abuse
____ used foul language or taken God's name in vain in order to hurt you
____ told you that God cannot save you from his abuse
____ tried to confuse your children by arguing against the Bible
____ other _____

Has another Christian (particularly a minister or Christian counselor):

____ told you that you are at fault for your husband's abusive behavior
____ told you that you must become more submissive
____ encouraged your husband to be abusive in his leadership
____ encouraged you to accept abusive behavior as "God's will"
____ encouraged you to rejoice in the abuse as your "cross" to bear
____ refused to help you to confront or to escape the abuse
____ known about the abuse, but chosen to ignore your plea for help
____ indicated that he believes your husband's abuse is God's punishment for your sins
____ other _____

47

Has the spiritual abuse resulted in your becoming:
____ convinced that you have no worth in God's eyes
____ afraid to attend church or fellowship with Christians
____ worried that your children will not be raised as Christians
____ convinced that you are not properly submissive because you can never please your husband
____ confused as to what is your sin, and what is your husband's
____ convinced that God is using your husband's abuse to punish you or to test you
____ worried that other Christians will reject you because of your husband's behavior
____ convinced that you could control the abuse if you were a better Christian
____ afraid to admit to a minister or counselor what is happening in your home
____ unable to pray because you are ashamed before God
____ unable to pray because you are angry at God
____ doubtful that God can (or will) help you escape the abuse
____ other _____

Use the list above to help you recognize what has happened to you spiritually. Chapter six will use this list to help you start to align yourself with Scriptural principles. In chapter nine, it will assist you in making your plan of action.

Chapter 5
Exploring Your Emotions

"And the peace of God, which passeth all understanding, shall keep your hearts and minds through Christ Jesus."
(Philippians 4:7)

Searching the Scriptures for verses dealing with emotions would be, I think, a lifelong task. Joy, anger, fear, hope, resentment, bitterness, contentment, betrayal, sadness, envy, confusion, disappointment, hatred, love, guilt, despair and peace are eloquently expressed by the people with whom God deals throughout the Bible. God patiently reveals not only that He has given us the capacity for these emotions, and so understands them, but also that He is able to show us how best to use our feelings without allowing them to use us.

We seem to have a mental list which labels some emotions as "negative": anger, guilt, sadness, fear. This viewpoint keeps us from realizing the fact that they are very much a part of us, designed and installed by our Creator. Consider, however, how very dangerous it would be if God had not given us the ability to think as well as feel. Without fear, for example, we would be likely to wander blithely into hazardous situations and conditions. Even our concepts of love are very narrow compared to God's definitions. Outlining and discussing some of these emotions may enable you to better understand what you experience with your emotions, and why. Then you can align these feelings with Scriptural principles.

.

49

Love

Paul's definition of charity gives us a view of the all-encompassing scope of God's caring, and a clear example of the type of love God would have us develop and share with others. In addition to godly love, spouses can develop a deep and abiding brotherly love, and can share in sexual expressions of love.

"Love suffers long and is kind; love does not envy; love does not parade itself, is not puffed up;

does not behave rudely, does not seek its own, is not provoked, thinks no evil;

does not rejoice in iniquity, but rejoices in the truth;

bears all things, believes all things, hopes all things, endures all things.

Love never fails."　　　　　　　(I Corinthians 13:4-8, NKJV)

Throughout the Bible, God indicates that some of the essentials of real love are self-control (Matthew 5:43,44), the willingness and desire to respect, serve, share with, forgive and encourage the loved one (Ephesians 4:1-3; I Peter 3:1-7; Galatians 5:13; Hebrews 10:24; Proverbs 10:12; Ephesians 4:16). People in a battering relationship often display different, even destructive, feelings, actions, and attitudes which they identify as love. Either spouse may form an addictive attachment which is substituted and mistaken for love. Like an addiction to drugs or alcohol, the abnormal dependency on another person can overtake rational thought and action, and encourage denial of the problem. As with any addiction, the dependency may escalate to become overwhelmingly destructive.

Such an addiction will manifest, typically, in two ways. One or both partners may believe that it is impossible to live without the other, that his or her identity is only complete within the bounds of the relationship. A partner may nearly worship the mate, displacing the Almighty as his or her first love. A dependent person may accept extreme abuse, refusing to confront the problems in the marriage, and offering excuses for the errant spouse's behavior simply because he or she cannot face attempting to break the addiction. Often, this spouse has highly romanticized fantasies of marriage and uses them to escape facing the reality of what occurs in the relationship.

The second manifestation may include behavior in which the dependent spouse will go to any lengths to control and imprison the mate in order to assure that he or she will never be abandoned. This dependency/addiction can become so severe that the person displays many of the same types of behavior seen in a substance abuser who is threatened with separation from alcohol or drugs: lying, manipulation, an attempt to gain even greater control, threats of self-destruction, paranoia (extreme and irrational fear), losing touch with reality.

God has given us a definition of true love and many guidelines for its application in our lives. Review carefully what type of love you feel for your husband, and what you believe he feels for you. Compare the attributes of godly love to those which are displayed in your marriage. You may see a pattern of addictive behavior rather than a progression toward more open and growing love. In a relationship which has included battering, addictive dependency can prevent one or both partners from initiating healthy changes and from exploring the freedoms and potential for growth provided by godly love.

Anger

Anger is a multi-faceted emotion, one which is both the cause of, and can be caused by, other emotions. In its causative role, it may involve physical, emotional, and spiritual aspects. Ephesians 4:26 tells us: "Be ye angry, and sin not." Obviously, the Lord does not judge the feeling of anger as much as He does its resulting actions, thoughts, and feelings.

In the preceding chapters, you may have become angry when you identified the types of abuse that have been common in your relationship. You may be wondering if you are sinful in your anger toward your husband and his behavior. You may have seen so much fury in him that you are afraid to acknowledge your anger with him for having mistreated you.

51

Although I hesitate to use the term "righteous anger," because some people would misuse it, I urge you to consider whether your anger might indeed be righteous in that it is an appropriate and healthy reaction to being victimized by your spouse. Physical, emotional, and spiritual abuse is wrong. He has chosen to act in hurtful and cruel ways, in rebellion to God's divine commands.

If you are angry that he has lost control, hurt you and the children, refused to take responsibilities which are rightly his—good for you! God does not condemn anger which is a reaction to injustice and to innately wrong behavior. Jesus was very angry at the Pharisees who had less concern for a man with a withered hand than for the letter of the law. " ... He when he had looked round about on them with anger, being grieved for the hardness of their hearts ... " (Mark 3:5).

Hand-in-hand with the recognition of this type of feeling goes outlining what you are doing or should do about the anger. During any phase of the cycle of violence, have you yourself lost control, screamed, hit or otherwise acted out your anger? Each of us is capable of violent behavior, and anger is one emotion which precipitates some very abusive actions. Anger causes insensitivity, fear of reprisals, guilt, depression, and many more feelings which are often expressed in ways which hurt ourselves or other people. However, repressing anger breeds bitterness, resentment, and hatred. Denying anger toward an abusive spouse can be dangerous in that it allows "sandbagging," a build-up of angry feelings which accumulate like interest on money in the bank. This provokes damaging pressure which decreases your ability to recognize and express what caused the anger. Some women in abusive relationships suffer from depression, ulcers, headaches, and many other illnesses which are, in reality, caused by unexpressed anger. Though Scripture condemns expressing anger in ways which are hurtful to others, God can and does provide ways in which you can release the anger and avoid its damaging effects.

Confrontation is a Biblically sound practice (Luke 17:3-5; Matthew 5:22-24; 18:15). When done in love, confrontation becomes an opening for each party to express concerns and grievances without an attempt to manipulate or abuse the other. There are three Scriptural principles upon which confrontation is based.

The first principle is that the one who confronts must do so in a spirit of love. Godly love has among its attributes that it hopes, covers, bears, believes, and perseveres in all things. Thus, a believer confronts with a willingness to resolve difficulties because she wants to remove the obstacles which unbalance the harmony of her relationship with the other person, whether it is professional or personal. Confronting in love removes the possibility that the confrontation becomes a personal attack or selfish manipulation.

Secondly, Scriptural confrontation must be done in the strength of Biblically sound doctrine. The confronter must have determined that her grievance or concern is the result of an action or attitude to which she has a right to object because God's word identifies it as inappropriate. Her own feelings must be examined in light of Scripture and through prayer. The decision to confront another person should be based upon a need to identify and resolve a conflict, confident that God's Word clearly dictates what is and is not acceptable. The confronter's own hurts or fears are less important than that both parties are able to reconcile their stand with God's perfect will.

Thirdly, the end result of confrontation must be left in God's hands. The confronter must be willing to accept that she can only express, appropriately, her concerns. She must listen in love and with a desire to understand what the other person says, yet with a firm belief in her right to disagree. She need not allow the other party to confuse or overpower her. Ultimately, she must have no preconceived ideas of "winning" or "losing"—concepts which have no place in confrontation. Instead, her goal should be to accurately and appropriately present her feelings, thoughts and possible solutions, to listen prayerfully to the other person's viewpoint, and to allow God to help her discern the validity of that viewpoint. Sometimes, two people will not resolve a problem because one or both want to win an argument. If both people lay aside defensiveness and work toward Scriptural resolution, God will provide a way for both to win and to grow.

It would be unwise to confront someone who is likely to harm you. If your husband would perceive a loving confrontation as a threat to which he must retaliate, you would be foolish to pursue that course. Instead, pray that God will arrange a proper time, and find other ways to express your anger appropriately.

If it is not safe to display your anger or pain to the other person, you can write down your feelings and use this as a medium of expression and as a prayer guide. Rigorous physical activity often helps to alleviate the stress you feel when you are angry. Develop some activities which you can rely on when you become angry.

Prayer is an ideal way to avoid committing a sin when you feel angry. Take a moment to pray, telling the Lord that you are angry and asking for help to express it properly. This will help to defuse your own anger. If the situation cannot be resolved at that time, perhaps because the other person is not willing to discuss the problem, you can avoid allowing resentment and bitterness to build by relying upon God to listen and respond to your needs. Prayer provides not only release of the tension, but the opportunity to listen to God's guidance in the situation. The Lord may show you how to be more compassionate and understanding, or He may lead you to confront a situation with wisdom and strength.

Anger can be the result of other emotions, too, a kind of rash which appears when something has abraded you. It is often much easier to act upon anger than to recognize someone else's power to hurt us. This type of anger, felt as a replacement emotion for others which are more difficult to name and accept, is a false feeling used as a shield for our most vulnerable areas: our feelings of self-worth and our fear of rejection.

Give careful thought as to what is likely to make you angry. Though many things cause angry feelings, the results of anger are completely within your control. Choose to express your anger in ways which do not hurt others or yourself, and in ways which provide for your own safety physically, emotionally, and spiritually. If you confront a person who is unlikely to become violent with a firm but calm demeanor and state that you are angry, willing to discuss why, and ready to help resolve the problem, it is likely that you will be able to avoid damaging behavior and still express your feelings. This would be in keeping with Ephesians 4:26,27: "Be ye angry, and sin not: let not the sun go down upon your wrath: neither give place to the devil."

Women in abusive relationships seldom have the opportunity to express any emotions without taking the chance that their spouses will react violently or use the information against them. Try to recognize your anger and use it constructively. That is, let anger motivate you to change the abusive relationship by confronting your spouse and demanding that he get help to change, or by leaving him to protect yourself, hopeful that this will move him to go for help. If you are in physical danger of injury or death from abuse, you have both the right and the obligation to seek protection. Two Scriptures clearly outline God's desire for us to shun actions, desires, attitudes or situations, both in ourselves and in others, which would cause us physical, emotional, and/or spiritual damage.

" . . . Behold, the fear of the Lord, that is wisdom; and to depart from evil is understanding" (Job 28:28).

The Lord tells us that to respect and revere Him is wisdom. Wisdom is the intelligent application of knowledge. He says that to depart from evil—to refuse to be a part of sin—is proof of the believer's comprehension that God values her as an individual. God desires His followers to stay away from that which would harm them. Avoiding danger knowledgeably is God-given wisdom.

Deuteronomy 6:16, Matthew 4:7, and Luke 4:12 also warn us, "Thou shalt not tempt the Lord thy God."

God does not look with favor on a believer who deliberately stands open to temptation or danger. The believer should not consent to someone's misuse of the Word of God or challenge

God's gracious provisions. Jesus Himself used Scripture to counter Satan's taunts and temptations.

Guilt

It is interesting to note that the more permissive our society becomes, the more guilt we seem to exhibit. It is a powerful emotion, closely tied to our spiritual perceptions and expressed in many ways.

Guilt is the product of what we call our conscience. This strict headmaster is constantly monitoring our behavior, attitudes, and beliefs to spotlight those which need attention. But often our consciences are manipulated by Satan and by other people, by culture and environment. The only one who should be able to approach our mind and emotions through our conscience is God. And sometimes He is the only one whose messages we fail to notice! If we explore guilt as having at least three possible origins, perhaps we can begin to identify and manage it in our lives.

There is a type of guilt which comes from God. He convicts those who will listen that something is out of alignment in their lives. He directs their attention toward the problem in a variety of ways, and demands two things from the guilty: a) confession of their wrongdoing, and b) repentance, or turning away from the sin. Confession to God strengthens your spiritual bond with Him and keeps an open path of communication between you and your Creator. Repentance is your acceptance of your responsibility to recognize and avoid continued transgression. God convicts us that we have disobeyed, and He provides forgiveness and direction in order to alleviate the guilt. Confessing our sins may bring immediate freedom, or God may direct us to take action which will rectify our wrongdoing and allow us to release the burden.

Although the Bible gives many specific examples of what is and is not permissible in a Christian's life, not all the guilt feelings you carry may be from sin in your life. It would be very tidy if you could label each item about which you feel guilty, identify what you did wrong, and confess it to God, making every effort to realign your will with His. Many Christians believe that it is that simple. But, if you are a woman involved in an abusive relationship, guilt may be an indefinable burden, a collection of false blame imposed on you by your husband and yourself.

If you have gone to God, ready and anxious to confess your guilt, only to find yourself confused as to what exactly you feel guilty about, you have probably picked up a burden of guilt and carried it without questioning whether or not you should accept it. An abusive husband encourages his wife to feel guilty for the turmoil in their family. When she accepts the responsibility for her spouse's behavior, he can continue to ignore his need to repent and change. This second type of guilt we carry is false guilt. It is guilt which we have failed to recognize as a manipulation of our feelings by others, not a conviction from God.

Society imposes unrealistic demands upon us. If we do not examine them carefully, we may find ourselves feeling guilty for not living up to its arbitrary standards. One of its most ridiculous demands is that women must somehow be more kind, loving, understanding, and forgiving than men or any other member of the family. The Bible does not make women more responsible for her children or husband than the husband is for his family. Yet often we feel guilty if our family is experiencing problems, or if we do not live up to its fictitious ideals of the ravishing woman, supermom, dedicated wife, loving daughter, ambitious career woman, devout Christian, immaculate housekeeper, ever-ready volunteer, and talented hobbyist. Much of the guilt that women assume is based upon unrealistic expectations imposed by a twisted, materialistic, secular society. This guilt feeling is often confused with conviction from God, and must be examined carefully.

Admittedly, this is a somewhat simplistic way to look at guilt, and does not explain or define many of its causes, but it may help you begin to explore how and why you feel guilty.

If your self-esteem is based upon the concepts of a society which admires beauty and wealth above honesty and concern for others, you have probably been at least mildly disappointed in yourself. Now try to perceive yourself as God does: as a unique individual who is loved unreservedly and who is capable of reflecting God's loving image. When you do, you will find that it is easier for you to refuse to accept what society tells you about your worth. Often we add to God's commandments an amazing number of irrelevant and petty standards which we force ourselves to try to follow. Some Christians are convinced that they must walk, talk, think, feel, or react within very rigid parameters. They condemn themselves daily for not meeting standards which God has not imposed, but which they believe will make them more acceptable, or prove that they are truly committed to God.

As you carefully analyze your feelings of guilt, try to determine if you have actually sinned by commission or omission. That is, have you done something wrong or not done something which was your responsibility? Try to be honest with yourself about what really is your responsibility, and what is something which others expect you to do out of possible selfishness or laziness on their part. Examine your own values to see if they are rigid or restrictive beyond what God has ordained.

If you feel guilty about abusive behavior in your family, explore what sins are involved. If your husband physically abuses you, he has sinned. If he abuses you and tells you that you caused him to beat you, can you really accept that responsibility? Short of taking his hand and applying it to your face, can you force your husband to strike you? Nothing can make him hit you if he chooses to control his actions. He can walk away, take a drive, call a friend. He has alternatives other than physical violence from which to choose. Most people can cite conditions under which they would not blame a man for striking his wife, but, in reality, nothing can *make* him hit her. It is always an act which he *chooses*. Control over our own actions is demanded by God. Proverbs 25:28 says, "He that hath no rule over his own spirit is like a city that is broken down, and without walls."

If your husband is verbally abusive, must you accept

everything he blames on you? Is every quality he pinpoints really one which you display? Refusing to accept such abuse and seeing yourself without his accusations will help to relieve some of the guilt you feel. If you have a close friend, ask her if she sees those qualities in you. You are human. You do have less than admirable traits. Work to improve those and refuse to accept labels which are maliciously hurled simply to hurt you.

"Woe unto them that call evil good, and good evil; that put darkness for light, and light for darkness; that put bitter for sweet, and sweet for bitter" (Isaiah 5:20). False accusations and manipulation can be refused by one who can discern them.

If your husband has abused you spiritually, you may feel guilty that you spend time at church, reading the Bible, or praying. Prayerful examination of the facts will help you to see that your spouse provokes this guilt as a way to manipulate you into giving up something which is vitally important to you. He may quote the Bible to prove your inadequacies, using your own faith in God's Word against you. Guilt imposed by someone deliberately trying to control you is neither God-given nor acceptable. "Let us not therefore judge one another any more: but judge this rather, that no man put a stumblingblock or an occasion to fall in his brother's way" (Romans 14:13).

Once you have sorted through the guilt feelings you carry, take the ones which rightfully belong to you and humbly go to God in prayer. There, you can release the weight of the burden, knowing that God will forgive you and provide the help you need to avoid repeating your transgressions.

Fear

As Christians, we are commanded to fear God, to hold Him in abiding respect, and to seek Him first in all things. The Bible refers to three other types of fear which we feel.

We approach cautiously things which present a danger to our bodies, minds, and spirits. A mother fears letting her child run into a busy street because there is a very real danger that the child could be hit by a car. This caution is healthy, based on information which is appropriately processed.

First John 4:18 says, "There is no fear in love; but perfect love casteth out fear: because fear hath torment. He that feareth is not made perfect in love." Perfect love is what God gives us, and it is in that perfect love that we trust. Tormenting fear cannot stand in the face of God's assurance that He is worthy of your trust. In a marriage filled with abuse, you may have learned that it is not safe to trust love, that it is best to reserve much of what you have to give so that you are less easily hurt when your trust is betrayed. That is the torment of fear. By trusting God to provide for your needs with unchanging and immovable love, you will begin to release the torment of fear, able to trust God and yourself.

Fear of failure keeps many people from attempting to change even the most dangerous areas of their lives. Have you ever thought about the experiences you consider as failures? Each of us has mental "success" and "failure" stickers which we put on our experiences and attempts. We might automatically affix a "failure" sticker to the time we interviewed for a job, but were not hired. We may do so without acknowledging that God had not planned for us to have that particular position. We stick a "failure" label on one of God's successes!

Dejected and self-pitying, we often position "failure" labels squarely in the middle of our foreheads. If, instead of marking our past experiences as "successes" and "failures," we prayerfully printed our mental labels with "learning experience," "remanded to prayer," and "forgiven by the Father," we would be better prepared to wear a "success in progress" label on our foreheads. Do not limit God's ability to work in your life by giving in to the fear of failure.

You may have fallen into the trap of assuming that if you don't try, you can't possibly fail. Other people may notice that you don't fail. God will notice if you don't try.

People who risk failure are not content to rest in whatever false security others find in the fear of failure. Courage does not spring out of fearlessness, but out of hope. It is the quality of looking disaster in the eye, and trying, not giving in to it. Pray for your courage to be strengthened. "For ye have not received the spirit of bondage again to fear; but ye have received the Spirit of adoption . . . " (Romans 8:15).

The third type of fear is harder to define because it exists as a vague but unsettling emotion, or as a rampaging, all-encompassing obsession. Paul wrote to his "dearly beloved son" Timothy, "For God hath not given us the spirit of fear; but of power, and of love, and of a sound mind" (II Timothy 1:7). The "spirit of fear" to which Paul refers is a general feeling of being unprotected, vulnerable, alone. Often we feel this way if we allow ourselves to drift away from close communication with God, neglecting to go to Him for reassurance and strength. If the abuse in your family leaves you feeling weak and lonely, it may be this spirit of fear which makes you forget that you are very important to God and capable of making decisions which will provide for your safety, your need for companionship, your goals and desires.

Perhaps you are afraid that you are going crazy. Some women who live in abusive relationships over long periods of time feel crazy, but it is a reaction to the stress and to their need to regain control of their lives.

Remember that "The spirit . . . of power, and of love, and of a sound mind" is promised to every believer. God will give you whatever strength you need, day by day, to change your life. You must rely on Him to meet every obstacle and to provide love, compassion, and understanding which enables you to move on. Worry and fear obscure His divine guidance. Uncertainty and confusion must give way to trust in God's omniscience and omnipotence.

Use the lists which detail the abuse you have endured to help you complete the following chart. These twelve questions and statements will help you to explore your feelings. Write down any other thoughts or ideas that you may have. These pages will then help you to make a plan of action.

How Do I Really Feel?

The first two questions must be studied in light of the Scriptural attributes of godly love. The Bible contains over five hundred references to love. Carefully consider some of these Scriptures and use them to help you determine what is the binding force in your relationship: Matthew 19:19; John 15:12; Romans 13:10; II Corinthians 5:14; Galatians 5:6; Ephesians 6:23; I Thessalonians 5:8; Colossians 2:2; I Peter 1:22; I John 3:18; I John 4:18; John 15:12; Acts 23:21; John 8:32; I John 4:21; Ephesians 5:28; Proverbs 15:12; Psalm 119:88; Psalm 40:10; Ephesians 4:2.

1a.) Can you identify some feelings you display toward your husband which are indicative of godly love?

1b.) Can you identify some feelings you display which may indicate that you have formed an addictive attachment?

2a.) Can you identify some feelings your husband displays toward you which are indicative of godly love?

2b.) Can you identify some feelings your husband displays toward you which may indicate that he has formed an addictive attachment?

3.) List actions, phrases or attitudes your husband may use or display that make you angry.

4.) Describe how you react or what you do when you are angry.

5.) List some of the things for which you feel guilty.

6a.) What would you like to do that you are not doing now?

6b.) List some of the fears which are holding you back from doing them.

7.) What do you think are your best:
 a.) physical attributes? (See Song of Solomon 4:1-5.)

 b.) emotional and intellectual qualities? (See Proverbs 31:10,13,16,17,18,20,25,26.)

 c.) spiritual gifts? (See I Corinthians 12:4-11 and 13:4-8.)

8.) What makes you happy?

9.) What do you resent or feel bitter about?

10.) Including God, who cares about you?

11.) What do you fear?

12.) For what are you most thankful?

Chapter 6
Scriptural Realignment

"O Lord, thou hast searched me and known me. Thou knowest my downsitting and mine uprising, thou understandest my thought afar off.... Search me, O God, and know my heart: try me, and know my thoughts: And see if there be any wicked way in me, and lead me in the way everlasting." (Psalm 139:1,2,23,24)

Realigning yourself with Scriptural principles may be a difficult task. In the first three chapters, I hope you noted the types of abuse occuring in your relationship and wrote down some ways abusive behavior has affected you. You may have a list of emotions you identify as the result of abuse, and some of these feelings will be hard for you to face. Admitting that you are angry, resentful or bitter may make you feel guilty. You may be confused as to whether or not these feelings and your own actions are sinful. God does not use just one verse, or a part of one verse, with which to realign His wandering children. We must view the Bible as a whole, willing to seek His will and testing our interpretations to assure that they hold constant with God's recurring themes. Over and over, in both the Old and New Testaments, God proves His desire to give us ways in which to align our will with His, to make decisions which rely upon His perfect guidance. He speaks to us as individuals, knowing each of us intimately, and never failing to supply what He knows we need.

Defining Sin

Though most Christians can give numerous definitions of sin, and many examples of sin in their own lives, it is important to focus on sin from God's viewpoint as well as our own. God used various words in the Bible which are translated as "sin." Reverend C.I. Scofield has provided a commentary on "the true nature of sin in its manifold manifestations."[1] In part, he identifies that: "Sin is *transgression,* an overstepping of the law and the divine boundaries between good and evil (Psalm 51:1; Luke 15:29); *error,* a departure from right (Psalm 51:9; Romans 3:23); *trespass,* the intrusion of self-will into the sphere of divine authority (Ephesians 2:1); *lawlessness,* or spiritual anarchy (I Timothy 1:9); *unbelief,* or an insult to divine truthfulness (John 16:9)." We are all guilty before God because of our sins, justified only by our acceptance of His gracious and merciful salvation provided through the death and resurrection of His Son, Jesus Christ.

In addition to the words above, consider the word "trap" as a synonym for sin. This is not an attempt to give sin a more acceptable or less guilt-producing name. Rather, God has warned us about thoughts, actions, and attitudes in our lives that are sinful, and has thus lit neon signs which warn us that they are traps which will affect us physically, psychologically, and spiritually. See Ephesians 6:11, I Timothy 3:7, and II Timothy 2:26.

Concerning Submission

Some of the questions asked most often by Christian women in abusive relationships pertain to the verses which deal with the submission of a wife to her husband. Ephesians 5:22 says, "Wives, submit yourselves unto your own husbands, as unto the Lord." In Colossians 3:18 we read, "Wives, submit yourselves unto your own husbands, as it is fit in the Lord." And I Peter 3:1 instructs, "Likewise, ye wives, be in subjection to your own husbands; that, if any obey not the word, they also may without the word be won by the conversation of the wives."

Each of these verses clearly commands the wife to place herself in submission to her husband. Each makes plain the fact that submission is a choice that the wife makes, one which she is to implement responsibly within the boundaries of proper authority and God's will. Each verse also qualifies or explains proper submission.

Paul says that a woman should defer to her husband in the same manner that the church submits itself to the Lord. In Ephesians 5:23 God appoints the man as the head of the wife, just as Christ is head of the church. A godly man will care for her as Christ cares for His beloved believers. By God's decree, she is guaranteed protection and lovingkindness. A man who understands and follows Christ's example is more concerned for his wife's well-being than for his own. Her submission to his loving authority would in no way endanger her physical, emotional, or spiritual safety. In such a marriage relationship, the woman is free to discuss her needs and ideas, knowing that her husband respects and cherishes her (Ephesians 5:28,29). Her husband would encourage and support her personal growth. She would trust his perceptions, seek his advice, respect his proper authority, and savor his companionship.

However, without the mutual respect for God's boundaries, this type of submission could be fatal for a woman who is married to an abusive man. Rather than pacifying her spouse, submission to his abuse often has the effect of granting him a "license to kill." The batterer gives himself permission to sin when he is angry or frustrated. A woman who accepts his abusive behavior, who submits to his irrational actions or attitudes, reinforces his belief that he has a right to his sin. He will continue to lose control because he does not need to learn other ways to express himself. The physically violent man can seriously injure or kill his wife. The emotional batterer can eventually kill his wife's spirit as well as her joy, contentment and self-concept. The spiritual abuser often dangerously damages his wife's Christian walk and frays her lifeline to her Saviour.

Trusting the Lord encompasses the knowledge that He is

capable of caring for us in ways beyond our expectations. Having provided His own Son as the sacrifice for my sins, He proves Himself as One who is willing and able to lead me justly and righteously. His nature is such that He cannot betray my trust. From this standpoint, when Paul demands that a woman trust her husband in the same way that she trusts the Lord, he further demands that her husband conduct himself in a trustworthy manner and be the same kind of spiritual head of his marriage as Christ is of the church.

In Colossians, Paul says that a wife's submission should be " . . . as it is fit in the Lord." We know that God does not want us to sin. A Christian woman is never called upon to sin, nor justified in sinning, in order to be submissive to her husband.

God has given us guidelines by which to judge what constitutes proper submission. He commands us to place ourselves in submission to His will. Thereafter, we are to be submissive to other designated authority as long as it does not violate His commandments. Each believer has a responsibility to submit to laws imposed by government (Matthew 22:21); to respect his or her church leaders (I Timothy 5:17), and to obey regulations set forth by an employer (II Thessalonians 3:10). Proper submission is always measured in light of what we know to be designated in God's Word.

We should not encourage others to sin by providing them even tacit permission or excuses. It is the responsibility of each believer to examine our own actions, to determine if they are in accord with God's Word, and to discern sinful behavior in others (Galatians 6:1). We should exercise wisdom and judgment to avoid submitting to a husband if it breaks other commandments. Submitting to a man engaged in repeated and unrepented sin would certainly not be right in the eyes of the Lord.

In both Ephesians and Colossians, Paul goes on to describe the individual obligations of husbands and wives. He addresses a Christian family and clearly calls on each person to assume a specific place in this relationship. Nowhere does he propose that a wife suffer at the hands of her husband. He does not imply that her position is like that of a slave or a beast of burden. Instead, he indicates that each person should serve the other. It is the mutual giving of husbands and wives which provides the foundations for the family of which Paul speaks.

Peter explains, in I Peter 3, that in being submissive a wife may influence her husband even if he is disobeying God. Since other Scriptures also affirm that our demeanor can prompt others to reassess their actions, we know that Peter advocates submission as an act which could persuade the husband to accept his proper role in the family. It is important for a wife to remember that allowing her husband to abuse her causes him to view her—and possibly her faith—with profound disrespect. Such disrespect is unlikely to help him want to behave more appropriately. Instead, he may use it as justification for treating her badly.

When a wife refuses to accept abusive behavior from her spouse, she is setting a good example. She provides him an opportunity to change his behavior for his own good and that of the family. This makes it possible for her to submit to his reasonable expectations for their lives and to support proper emotional outlets should he decide to control his abusive behavior.

God commands that each believer act in ways which he or she knows to be in line with His Word, and to refuse to participate in anything which breaks His commands. A Christian woman must recognize that physical, emotional, and spiritual abuse to her or her children is sin. If her husband is sinning, she has no obligation to accept his behavior and risk injury. *To remain in a relationship which involves severe or frequent abuse is to allow a batterer to continue to sin and to avoid facing the consequences of his behavior.*

Biblical submission must also be viewed in light of the Scripture which tells us that our bodies are to be temples of the Holy Spirit (I Corinthians 6:19). As vessels of the Creator, we are obligated to protect ourselves reasonably in order to be able to fulfill what God has ordained for us. Allowing another person to abuse our bodies, minds, and spirits can effectively short-circuit our ability to use them in God-directed ways.

Reconciling the Past

Some of the guilt we carry may have been a burden for much of our lives. If you were told as a child that everything you did was wrong or not quite good enough, you probably began to carry burdens of guilt long before you entered your present relationship. If your father was abusive toward your mother, or toward you or other children in the family, you began to learn at an early age how to be a victim. The skills which you developed for coping with anger, fear, and rejection were those which made it easier to live in a violent home.

Although it is common that a batterer's background includes domestic violence, (he may have seen his mother beaten or have been abused himself), women who become victims of abuse do not necessarily come from abusive homes. However, most women in our society have been taught that women should not be assertive or demanding. Most have been raised to be nurturers, to accept the major responsibility for keeping their homes and families neatly in order. Until recent times, it was unusual for women to step out of their traditional roles and to explore new areas in which to exercise other possibilities. In our society, men most often assume the dominant role at home and in the workplace.

Most victims of domestic violence hold very traditional ideas concerning the home and family. While these roles should be respected and preserved, women are often stereotyped, and sometimes given little credit as to the multitude of other talents and abilities they have. Many myths evolve out of these stereotypes. It is myth that women are weak, that they need a marriage license as a man's "stamp of approval," that marriage validates their worth, or that women are less capable than men of succeeding in a chosen profession.

In an abusive relationship, a batterer will often demand that his wife remain in stereotypical roles in order to assure himself that he is superior to her. He also attempts to insure that she feels unable to leave him, no matter what he does to her. Look closely at your relationship. You may have fallen into a pattern of living as a victim. You may find it difficult to say "no" to people, or to let them know that you are displeased, angry, or unwilling to accept their behavior toward you. You can release the anger, guilt, and fear and begin to decide what is right for you in your own life if you are willing to explore some of these feelings, and to take steps to help yourself without doing damage to others. This, in itself, is difficult to manage. Your husband, children, mother, father, and others may choose to take offense when you begin to change your behavior. They may label you selfish, crazy, or silly when you refuse their demands or set limits on what you will accept from them.

The abuse which you have endured may be a weight in your heart that you feel unable to relieve. You may be bitter and resentful toward your husband and wonder how to release the burden of years of abuse. There are seven steps which will help you begin to reconcile the past and to focus on the future.

1. *Ask forgiveness for past sins.* Lay your hurts, guilts and fears at God's feet. Sort through your burdens and ask God to show you those which are rightfully yours, and to discard those which are not yours to confess. Go daily to the Father, remembering that no one can understand as He can, no one can ease your pain as He can, no one can give you forgiveness as He can. *Be ready to accept forgiveness and be ready to forgive the hurts done to you. Remember that forgiveness is not an emotion, but an act of your will.* You need not minimize the things which others have done to you; you need not deny that you know someone else's action or word was sinful and that it caused you pain. Simply ask God to help you forgive the past as a way of reflecting His image, as a way of giving glory to His willingness to forgive, and as an act of faith that God's judgment and righteousness will prevail, releasing you from bitterness and resentment. "If we confess our sins, He is faithful and just to

forgive us our sins, and to cleanse us from all unrighteousness" (I John 1:9).

2. *Accept that the past is unchangeable.* Decide that you will explore the past as a way of changing the future. File the hurts and ruined dreams in a folder marked "experience" and use it to help, instead of hurt, yourself. Pray for insight into your past that will allow you to be strengthened by what God has helped you overcome. "And all things are of God, who hath reconciled us to himself by Jesus Christ, and hath given to us the ministry of reconciliation" (II Corinthians 5:18).

3. *Make worksheets which put your concerns plainly in front of you.* You will find sample worksheets in each chapter of this book. They can help you to explore how the information in each chapter relates to your situation. They will aid you in praying specifically for God's intervention, wisdom and comfort. "Remembering without ceasing your work of faith, and labour of love, and patience of hope in our Lord Jesus Christ, in the sight of God and our Father" (I Thessalonians 1:3).

4. *Begin to break out of "solitary confinement."* If you have no close friends, little contact with people outside your home, or can't seem to develop friendships with people in your church, neighborhood or at work, take steps to reach out to others and establish some links. This is risky, and you may be afraid of rejection, but finding even one person with whom to share will give you a new feeling of freedom. Ask God to help you find a kind and loving friend with whom to fellowship. "It is of the Lord's mercies that we are not consumed, because his compassions fail not" (Lamentations 3:22). "A man that hath friends must shew himself friendly" (Proverbs 18:24).

5. *Find and write down verses which comfort you.* Those which speak to you personally will motivate you to align yourself with God's will. My favorite comfort verse is Psalm 138:7,8 which says, in part, "Though I walk in the midst of trouble, thou wilt revive me . . . The Lord will perfect that which concerneth me." If you find a Scripture while reading, hear one in a sermon or while talking to a friend, write it down and then read the chapter that contains that verse. Memorize those that

are particularly dear to you and repeat them to yourself when you need support and guidance. "Thy word have I hid in mine heart, that I might not sin against thee" (Psalm 119:11).

6. *Be willing to wait for God's answers, knowing that He will bring about His perfect plan in its time.* While it may be important to act quickly in matters of safety, do not rush into decisions without prayerful consideration. "Wait on the Lord, and keep His way, and he shall exalt thee to inherit the land" (Psalm 37:34). See also Proverbs 21:5 and 16:20.

7. *"Wherefore take unto you the whole armour of God,* that ye may be able to withstand in the evil day, and having done all, to stand. Stand therefore, having your loins girt about with truth, and having on the breastplate of righteousness; And your feet shod with the preparation of the gospel of peace; Above all, taking the shield of faith, wherewith ye shall be able to quench all the fiery darts of the wicked. And take the helmet of salvation, and the sword of the Spirit, which is the word of God: Praying always with all prayer and supplication in the Spirit . . . " (Ephesians 6:13-18).

These are your keys to reconciling the past, and an important part of preparing for the future. Humiliation, fear, guilt, anger, temptation, failure, and worry may have wounded us because some part of our armor has slipped or been left behind. We are all vulnerable when we neglect to use God's protective provisions: truth, our defense against confusion; righteousness, which wards off fear; the preparation of the gospel of peace, armor against weariness as we trod a narrow path; the shield of faith, by which we turn away doubt and reflect assurance and hope; the helmet of salvation, our acceptance of the gift and the knowledge of the price Christ paid to make us worthy; the sword of the Spirit, the guiding force which is able to repel attackers.

Take time to look carefully at each piece of armor available to you. Keep it in battle-ready condition, knowing that God has designed each piece perfectly for your protection.

Commandments, Rights and Privileges

We all know about the ten commandments in which God identified a code of good and evil, right and wrong. Whether or not we fully understand those commandments is debatable. Though we know that these commandments were God's law, and that Jesus came to fulfill that law, we often forget that He did not change the commandments. He explained them more fully and enabled us to recognize the difference between God's judgment and our own limited perceptions. "Think not that I am come to destroy the law, or the prophets: I am not come to destroy, but to fulfill" (Matthew 5:17). And in Romans 13:9,10 Paul reminds us that love is the fulfilling of the law. The ten commandments are still powerful guidelines for our lives. Reread them and explore some of the misconceptions you may have about what they say (Exodus 20:1-17). Through Christ we are released from condemnation for our transgression of these laws. "For the law of the Spirit of life in Christ Jesus hath made me free from the law of sin and death" (Romans 8:2).

As you read the commandments, try to remember at least one example in Jesus' ministry which is based on that commandment. Try to understand how Jesus chose to teach on the law. Jesus used kindness, firmness, and understanding toward those who listened to Him. He did not waver in what He knew to be the letter of the law, but He also chose to explain what the spirit of that law encompassed. We must follow Christ's lead in combining law—its restrictions, directions and consequences—and love—for God, ourselves and others—in order to balance our lives.

As a believer, one of your responsibilities is to judge yourself and others without condemnation. "Judge not according to the appearance, but judge righteous judgment" (John 7:24). Righteous judgment involves acknowledging that a person's actions or words may be sinful, without condemning that person because of the sin. We are not even to condemn ourselves when we sin, but to repent and turn away from the sin. In righteous judgment, you weed out false guilt and inappropriate fear. You follow God's Word in both letter *and* spirit

75

because you do not neglect your own responsibilities, nor do you accept the burden of responsibilities which belong to other people.

You may believe that you have few rights as a Christian; that your life is to be barren of happiness, controlled by the shoulds and should nots of legalism. But God has given the Christian great power and liberty, clearly defining your rights as a child of the Father. He has not left you without spiritual swords and shields, without the ability to live well and happily. He combines rights and responsibilities to give you the strength to act on His direction. You have the right to go to God in prayer, unafraid of condemnation, fully expecting forgiveness and comfort because God has promised to be faithful and just (I John 1:9). Your safety is in the Lord (Proverbs 21:31b). But because your body is the temple of the Lord, you have an obligation to protect yourself from damage to your body, mind, or spirit in healthy ways. God will stand behind the decisions you have brought before Him in prayer, examined carefully, and made without malice toward others (Ephesians 4:30-32).

The Constitution of the United States declares that each person is endowed by God "with certain inalienable rights, and that among them are life, liberty and the pursuit of happiness." Consider what those words mean to you as a citizen! You have a right to live as an individual, free from bondage or entrapment, and to seek that which is precious to you, providing you do not infringe upon another's rights. If a group of men could show such great wisdom in defining and declaring each person's God-given rights, how much better must the Creator be able to outline His gifts to us?

Your privileges as a child of God are much like your rights, but may be different for each Christian. While your godly rights are also inalienable, your privileges are dependent upon the particular gifts which God has given you. You may have the privilege of serving the Lord in a particular ministry: music, child care, working with the elderly, as a speaker or a missionary. You may be privileged to have the gift of laughter, of compassion, of understanding others.

If you have lived for long in an abusive relationship, though, you may feel bereft of privileges. You may have surrendered many of your rights because of your husband's abuse, stopped using many of your known talents and kept yourself from exploring new privileges the Lord may be waiting to show you.

God's Word provides concrete commandments which form the foundation of responsibility for our lives. The rights with which He endows us are the solid structure which stands upon the foundation, able to weather storms and free to take shape as He wills. Our privileges are the beautiful furnishings within the structure, each unique, each useful and pleasurable. Again, our three interrelated parts, the body, mind and spirit, are fashioned to work for and with Him.

Prayer is the Lifeline

Prayer is one of the most gracious of His gifts. God the Creator, the Redeemer, and King of Kings invites each one of us to come before His throne, and there He welcomes us, instructs us, comforts, and forgives us. Satan, the accuser, cannot follow us there. His lies and deceitful ways lose their power as we rest in the safety and peace of our mighty God. No wonder Paul tells us to "pray without ceasing" (I Thessalonians 5:17). If we remain in an attitude of open communication with God, we are never alone and need never feel as if no one is listening.

Prayer is one of the best habits you can form. Proverbs 18:10 tells us that just the name of the Lord is a strong tower offering safety to those who run to it. If you can set aside a few minutes each day in which you can devote all your attention to communicating with God, you will begin to rely more fully upon His strength and to experience His peace. Throughout the day, begin to offer short prayers of praise, or to ask for help in even the smallest matter. The more you rely upon God's will to provide for your every need, the stronger and more capable you will become. Prayer is a give-and-take involvement with the One who never fails. You give your burdens to the Lord, admitting that you cannot bear them, and the Lord will take whatever you release to Him. You give Him thanks and praise for His provisions, and He increases His blessings. You give Him guilt and fear, and He pours out forgiveness and peace.

Before the throne of God you are accepted fully, completely, and enthusiastically as God directs His special attention on your spirit. We often allow ourselves to be intimidated by others whom we consider to be superior in some way to ourselves. We view their wealth or status, education or knowledge, position or power, and think ourselves unworthy. We feel less than competent compared to them. In the sight of God, though, we are all individuals desperately in need, and He is always willing to provide for that need, knowing our most secret thoughts and desires, and able to love us unreservedly. When you pray, be mindful of the enormous blessing you have in being able to approach God, cleansed by the blood of Jesus, an heir to Heaven by His righteousness. Not only may you approach God, but you may call Him Father, and ask anything in the name of your Saviour. If you pray with thought to the enormity of what God allows you, you will begin to better understand how very much He loves you, how very precious you are to Him. Reliance upon God will strengthen your self-esteem and assure you that the One upon whom you lean is immovable. You will be able to affirm that "I can do all things through Christ which strengtheneth me" (Philippians 4:13).

A prayer diary is an excellent way to discipline your prayer life. Any notebook will work. You can organize your prayer requests daily or weekly. Refer to the lists you have made of the abusive behavior in your family. Be very specific in praying for yourself, your children, your spouse, and others. Jot down Scripture passages which address the concerns you have and let them enhance your prayers. Ask God to reveal their wisdom more fully. The diary should also have a place in which to write down answers to prayers. Having a record of how and when God answers specific prayers will strengthen your faith and allow you to offer special praise and thanks for those answers.

When praying, pay special attention to your mental and spiritual attitudes. Choose a time when you are not rushed, or

can put aside other thoughts and matters while you talk to God.
Then be willing to listen, allowing God's peace and message to
reach your heart and mind. Perhaps you will be able to relate to
the way in which God is willing to wait for you to resign your will
to His gentle care in the following poem.

Nearly All . . .

Father, I am rushed and soon must hurry on my way.
*There's so much I need to do, and yet so much that I
should say.*
*Lord, You know I have been angry, have been tossed about
today.*
Forgive me, Lord.
I guess that's all I have to say . . .
or nearly all . . . .

Father, I am weary and afraid. Please understand!
*All I'm sure of is that nothing seems to go as I had
planned.*
*Lead me safely through this storm, and keep me gently in your
hand.*
Thank you, Lord.
I guess that's all I have to say . . .
or nearly all . . . .

*Oh, Father! I find my family is troubled, and I have no peace of
mind.*
*We need help to heal the wounds, loving care that's strong and
kind.*
Touch us, Lord.
I guess that's all I have to say . . .
or nearly all . . . .

Now, Father, I can feel that what I need is to be here.
Nothing else is as important, and I'm ready to draw near.
Teach me, Lord, and I will listen, search my heart and dry my
tears.
Praise you, Lord, for wanting me to give you all . . . not just
nearly all.

Catherine Scott

FOOTNOTES

[1] Definitions of sin from *The Scofield Reference Bible* edited by Rev. C.I. Scofield © 1909, 1917, 1937 and 1945 by Oxford University Press.

Chapter 7
Misplaced Manhood:
The Battering Husband

"His mischief shall return upon his own head, and his violent dealing shall come down upon his own pate." (Psalm 7:16)

The last few chapters have, necessarily, been focused almost entirely on you and your feelings, your relationship with God, and the types of abuse you might be experiencing. In this chapter we turn to the profile of the man who batters.

The batterer is a man caught in the fury of his cycle of violence. The stereotype of the abusive man as uneducated, a lower class drunkard, a loudmouth, or bullying hulk of a man is not always accurate. Violent men can be of any race, size, age, religious conviction, and social class. Men who are abusive to their wives and/or children may be respected businessmen, hardworking laborers, teachers, ministers, counselors, or have a high level of education. The common thread which weaves through the fabric of the batterer is not who or what he is in his community or church. Christian or non-Christian, rich or poor, educated or illiterate, the batterer is a man who uses abusive words and actions in an attempt to control those around him and to express his own inner turmoil.

The question which most wives of violent men want answered is *WHY* does he act that way? In order to truly understand it, we must look at our society, consider how a man often displays low self-esteem, and explore his anger, fear, and guilt. Then we can look at God's Word concerning true manhood and what He intended that to encompass.

Let's look first at some of the characteristics of batterers.

Charming And Deadly: Dr. Jekyl/Mr. Hyde

Some wives have difficulty convincing friends, family, his co-workers, or church members that her husband can become brutal. Many men who batter their wives are charming, attractive, and seemingly easygoing. Many battered wives can relate stories of his wit, his thoughtfulness, or his ability to attract people. Many tell me that if I met their husbands, I would probably like them, and they are often right.

During your courtship, you probably thought you had found Mr. Wonderful. Kind, courteous, thoughtful, romantic Mr. Right offered you love and a life of security and sharing. He may have seemed overly jealous, but perhaps that seemed to have a bit of old-fashioned charm. Perhaps it verified for you that his love was sincere. Was he easily angered, but quick to cool off and apologize?

At some point before or after your marriage, you probably began to see the potential for violence and to see the cycle begin. You might have mistaken his tension-building phase for simple nervousness, or assumed that you had failed to realize how much stress he had been under at work. The first abuse, whether it was physical, emotional or spiritual, may have seemed so out of character for him that you were shocked. And, during the loving aftermath, you might have been sure that he would never allow himself to be so cruel again.

The Controlling Batterer

While all batterers use anger to control others, this type of man has a need to exert his will over you in almost every area. He cannot accept that anyone else should be recognized as being as capable or farsighted as he. From the first, you may have considered him strong and positive, a very directed and "together" person. Perhaps you felt safe in accepting his suggestions, protected by his willingness to always be the decision-maker. But, when you first dared to disagree or to disobey, he retaliated with a fury you found alarming. He may have taken more and more control over the family finances and activities. Before long, it probably became clear that he expected to be in control of every aspect of your life, and you no longer felt flattered by his concern.

If you live with a controller, you may be frightened and resentful because you are not allowed to grow or to change. Instead, you are expected to remain within a narrow sphere of what he deems appropriate, wise, or permissible in your life. It is common for a controller to subtly change his demands in order to ensure that you will never be able to fully comply. These contradicting or additional demands give him destructive leverage in the relationship by forcing you to constantly fail.

Many times the controlling batterer uses threats to gain the upper hand. If your husband has threatened to kill you, the children, or himself if you leave him, you must take the threat seriously. These men can be capable of extreme violence in order to force others to comply with their will. While these threats should not keep you from leaving a violent relationship, you must exercise extreme caution in planning *how* you are to leave. Do not hesitate to seek police protection, restraining orders, or other professional help to ensure your safety. If you believe he could become suicidal, try to find a friend, pastor or family member who could help him through the first impact of your leaving. Do not jeopardize yourself or the children by telling anyone your whereabouts if you do not trust them to remain silent.

The Alcoholic Batterer

As we explore the types of men who batter, we find that their characteristics often combine or overlap. The alcoholic who beats his wife often has many of the characteristics of the sober batterer. If he is not a daily drinker but is given to periodic bouts of drunkenness, the alcoholic batterer may have long periods of sobriety. He may not show his violent tendencies while sober. If he only becomes abusive during his bouts of drinking, it is easy for his wife to blame the violence on alcohol. She may have little fear of him when he is sober. But, it is important to realize that he does not beat her because he loses control while drunk. Rather, he feels himself losing control, and gets drunk to avoid dealing with his stress and to give himself permission to act abusively.

If you live with an alcoholic, you know that his patterns of drinking and abusive behavior often coincide. Both drinking and brutality are ways that these men choose to deal with their emotional problems. Alcoholism and battering are behavioral disorders which characteristically stem from low self-esteem and an inability to use non-destructive ways to cope with stress. Both can be learned behavior, patterns which carry over from generation to generation.

The wives and children of alcoholics have found help, encouragement, and renewed hope through programs designed to address the pain involved in living with an alcoholic. Ask your minister if he knows of any Christian counselors who have support groups for the families of alcoholics. Al-anon and Al-ateen are two secular organizations which teach survival techniques based on education and group support to give a lifeline to families drowning in a spouse's or parent's alcoholism.

The Psychotic Batterer

I am not qualified to give a mental health professional's viewpoint on all the aspects of what might be identified as psychotic behavior. I believe that few batterers fall into this category. Most are men who need help to reassess the way in which they act on their emotions.

Researcher and sociologist Murray A. Straus indicates that he believes the percentage of psychotic woman abusers to be no greater than the percentage of psychotic people in the society at large, perhaps two to three percent. [1] Such severe mental disturbances might be identified in persons who enjoy inflicting pain, those who feel they are outside of society's boundaries and laws, and those who believe themselves directed by "voices" to harm or even kill their families.

There are several types of severe disturbances which can trigger violent behavior in which the person is entirely incapable of controlling his or her actions. Such people are often termed "criminally insane," and require intensive therapy, not simply the assistance of a counselor. The use of drugs and alcohol can eventually produce types of psychotic behavior.

Many Christian women have asked me if it is possible that their husbands are possessed by demons. They do not ask this in jest, nor are they being anything but honest when they wonder if "something else" takes over their husbands' bodies when the men are so out of control. As a Christian, I believe what the Bible tells us about the existence of demons and the influence that they can have over humans who are not aware of demonic power or those who seek to use their power. The Bible identifies the struggle Christians have: "For we wrestle not against flesh and blood, but against principalities, against powers, against the rulers of the darkness of this world, against spiritual wickedness in high places" (Ephesians 6:12).

I walk a fine line here between confirming the *possibility* of an abusive spouse being possessed, and looking frankly at the *probability*. If your husband is a Satanist, or is interested in or performs occult rituals, I must admit that I believe he is inviting demonic influences. If you are aware that your husband is involved in the occult, I suggest you seek special help from a minister who is knowledgeable in this area. You must be careful to choose a Bible-believing pastor who is experienced both in counseling and in dealing Scripturally with problems related to the occult. Perhaps your own minister can refer you to such a counselor, or you can contact a Christian counseling service for a referral. You can then explore the occult-related dangers in addition to the counseling you may seek to help end the abuse in your home.

Again, most men who batter are relatively healthy people

who need to explore and utilize alternate methods to handle anger and other emotions. The man who deals in the occult world is more severely troubled and needs, I believe, both spiritual and emotional therapy.

The Man the Victim Loves

Somewhere inside each of these batterers is the man his wife has loved. Perhaps she still feels that love, or maybe it is buried under resentment, fear, or anger because of the abuse she has taken. In phase three, she is most likely to see at least a shadow of the loving, romantic, giving man with whom she thought she could share her life.

Your husband may be devastated by his phase two behavior. And when he tells you how very sorry he is for having hurt you, he probably means it. He is ashamed, and may cry for your forgiveness. He may threaten to harm himself because he believes he cannot live without you.

It is often difficult for a battered wife to understand that most abusive men are extremely dependent upon their wives. If his love for you is based on fear and feelings of inadequacy, it is an addictive dependency, not an emotional bond to be shared. Part of your husband's need to control you may stem from his fear of losing you. Though he may appear to be very strong and self-sufficient, a man who abuses his wife is often convinced that he must possess his wife in order to be a complete person. This is one reason that a batterer sometimes becomes desperate enough to kill his wife rather than allow her to leave.

An abuser will not usually seek help for his behavior unless he inflicts life-threatening injuries and is arrested for assault or unless his wife has left him. He is probably good at denying the extent to which he abuses his family. He wants desperately to blame his wife, children, job, drinking, or anything but himself for the abuse. Men will go so far as to blame the wife for her injuries because she bruises so easily!

Is the man you love still there? Can he stop his behavior

before he kills you? Can you ever learn to trust him again? I don't know.

Without help from someone who understands and can approach this problem honestly and capably, there is a good chance that he will never learn to regain control. With prayer, and support from a knowledgeable counselor, he has the opportunity to re-educate himself to avoid abusive behavior. The man you see in phase three will not continue to be loving, or kind or remorseful unless he will ask God, and other people, to help him make the right choices.

The Battered Boy/The Battering Man

Violent men most likely learned violent behavior as children. Attitudes concerning violence, a woman's place in the family, the value of children, mutual respect between spouses, and the need for control are all learned, to a great extent, in our homes.

If you have any contact with your husband's parents, have you noticed how his father treats his mother? Is he verbally abusive, quick to berate her for a mistake? Have you ever seen him strike her? Your husband may have supplied details about his home life. He may tell stories in which he characterizes his father as angry or controlling, and his mother as weak or stupid. This will give you a good basis for understanding why it is so easy for him to fall into an abuser's role in your relationship.

Society as a whole has also done its part in shaping men into batterers. A man's duties as a provider, a protector, and an authority figure have been given more status than his role as a helper and nurturer. From the time they are babies, boys are expected to be rougher, tougher, less emotional, and more in control than girls. Boys are urged to compete, and often their competition is overseen by an adult raised in the same mold, unable to explain that winning the game is not the only possible victory.

The boy who receives the message "might makes right" from both his parents and society is warped into believing that his manhood depends upon being able to manipulate others by brute force. Even Christian families will often show the boy that he is somehow more valued than a daughter, or his father may quote Scripture while demeaning or physically abusing his wife and children. The boy begins to take pieces to the puzzle, and soon puts together a destructive and unbalanced picture. He *knows* that men must be superior to women, and so must be in a position to control them. He rationalizes that men must not show fear or loneliness, sadness or confusion.

What veneer does he choose to cover these feelings? The one which his parents and society have told him is acceptable: anger. Anger shows strength, he thinks. Anger is a cloak under which he hides the emotions he perceives as unacceptable or unmanly. And anger can be used to create the illusion that he is able to control his wife and children. He may manipulate them to avoid having to display honest feelings or to avoid the compromise with others normal in a balanced life.

To Own You Is To Love You

The batterer's family and his society may have also instilled in him a deep disrespect for women. Perhaps he saw his mother unable to stop his father from beating him and was angered that she didn't protect him from his father. He might have seen her as too weak to stand before his father's strength.

Or, his mother may have been the abusive parent. Because he could not respect and admire his mother's feminine qualities, the ungodly view of women being innately inferior to men was easily accepted. Society's treatment of women as sexual objects contributes to his disrespect. Pornography reinforces the depraved and dehumanizing view of women as "natural" victims to men's aggressions.

Often, a woman discovers that the batterer sought not a wife in the true sense of the word, but a piece of property. He never learned the difference between *loving* and *owning* people. If his disrespect for women is deeply seated, he will easily convince himself that all women are untrustworthy. His extreme jealousy and possessiveness can stem from this disrespect, as well as from his lack of adequate self-esteem.

His Self-Esteem

The batterer is often a wounded spirit. Child abuse, neglect, an alcoholic parent, and uncompromising discipline all leave scars which burn deeply into a person's concept of his own worth. He may have ridiculously high goals or expectations for himself which lead to constant frustration or disappointment. He may want to feel superior to women, or even other men, but is often threatened because they don't appear to honor his "superior" position. Even his children cannot exhibit the degree of respect he feels he must have to prove his worth. The man who feels he must use threats, insults, or physical abuse to control his family is saying that he will go to any lengths to avoid seeking solutions to problems within himself. A man does not degrade his wife, keeping her a prisoner to his desires, in the spirit of love. He does not slap her because he loves her, or for her own good. He does it to prove to himself, and perhaps to others, that he is "man enough to handle her."

The man who seeks counseling for his abusive behavior is in for a rough time emotionally. He will have to face his feelings without their protective veneer of anger. These emotions are threatening to him because he has a need to be strong, and he may perceive feelings as a weakness in his defenses. As we explore his emotional make-up, we will see how his spiritual and physical natures are also affected.

His Emotions

Anger is the emotion most often linked in our minds with the violent man. Often, anger is just a cover-up for other emotions he cannot express. Fear, jealousy, rejection, helplessness, and loneliness can all be manifested as anger. His anger may be directed at himself, but he turns it outward toward his family. He may use anger as a defense against being questioned or having to justify his actions. Anger is often a tool that the batterer can use to browbeat his spouse into submission, thereby allowing him to assume the superior stance he so desperately feels he needs. Anger may be the only emotion that he can freely express; the only way he knows of sharing pain or confusion.

Again and again we have seen the issue of control. But the emotion underlying this need in the batterer is fear. He is afraid, and this fear can be the spark which ignites his anger. It can be the reason he wants everyone around him to focus on him. Fear can motivate him to hurt even the people he loves in order to escape his own inadequacies. He is afraid that inside he is not as strong as he should be, not as capable, or smart, or worthy of love.

The violent man often feels tremendously guilty. He may have allowed society to convince him that he is not the achiever he should be. He may feel guilty that he has not provided a more luxurious home, become better educated, or more socially adept. Usually, men are quick to tie dollar amounts to the coattails of self-esteem. How much money he makes, or doesn't make, can have a great deal to do with how good he feels about himself. As his battering continues, he feels guilty for his actions. He may deny to you that he is an abuser, but may experience great difficulty in overcoming his knowledge that he lost control and betrayed your trust. Guilt often produces defensiveness, and defensiveness generates anger. The batterer who feels guilty spins back into the cycle because it helps him to release his frustrations.

Physically, the abuser focuses on his strength and how he can use it to manipulate others. Even a man who is only abusive verbally is aware on some level that the mere threat of using his superior strength puts him at an advantage over his wife. He knows, consciously or subconsciously, that she will accept his emotional mistreatment in the hope of not pushing him into actual physical abuse.

The batterer is no different from anyone else involved in continuing sin. He is digging a hole for himself spiritually. He deepens the hole each time he chooses to sin, and as the hole becomes deeper, the light becomes more dim. It becomes harder and harder for him to ask God for help because he digs relentlessly into his chosen pit.

I have not addressed, to any degree, the difference between the Christian batterer and his unsaved counterpart. It is certainly not because a Christian man cannot, or will not, be abusive to his wife. Many Christian men, including ministers, have dug into the rocky soil of abuse. Nor do I believe that a man who is unsaved would not benefit from counseling designed to help him control his violence. I have chosen not to differentiate between the two to any great extent because I have found that their actions are much the same. Saved or unsaved, these men beat their wives, call them filthy names, abuse and molest their children. The issues of their self-esteem and most of the solutions to their problems will be much alike.

The major differences between Christian and non-Christian men who batter will be in your approach to them. The Christian man who is willing to search Scripture with you in order to understand God's plan for your relationship will be confronted by his sin and forced to seek God's help in solving his problem. He has already accepted the saving blood of Christ. In doing so, he reached out to the Saviour in repentance for his sins, and he has the opportunity now to reach for forgiveness and cleansing from his failure to remain in God's will. He should be supported by other men and women in his church who can pray, exhort, and, if needed, admonish him to grow into proper manhood. Jesus gave us wonderful examples of strength, kindness, empathy, and proper ways to express our feelings. Men are told in Ephesians 5:25, "Husbands, love your wives, even as Christ also loved the church, and gave himself for it." A wife who removes herself from an abusive home, or confronts the batterer with help from their pastor or a Christian counselor, allows him to begin to reconstruct the position he has as a godly husband.

The unsaved man who has a Christian wife will probably resent interference from a minister or other church members.

He is likely to continue his abusive behavior even after having been confronted by church representatives. Because he has never experienced the confession and repentance of sin which begins every new believer's walk with the Lord, it may be more difficult for him to recognize and acknowledge his problem. The Christian woman may put herself in great danger if she preaches, or attempts to admonish her husband by using Scripture. He probably sees her faith as a threat to him, and using it to confront him with his abusive behavior could be literally fatal.

If you must leave in order to protect yourself, you can then begin to witness to your spouse about the reality of forgiveness in Christ, either on the phone or by letter. If your husband is involved in occult practices, however, be aware that it can be dangerous to confront him with Scripture. You may want to leave it to a counselor skilled in this area.

Regaining True Manhood

You have probably spent a great deal of time praying for safety, for solutions, and for your husband to turn from his violence. Perhaps you daydream about a family where no one deliberately hurts or hits someone else. Reality and our dream world often have nothing in common, but it *is* possible to have a family in which there is mutual respect and an orderly existence. It *is* possible to have a family in which both the husband and the wife are able to share ideas, feelings, situations, and even opposing opinions, and to grow through the sharing. This is not a fantasy but a reality in God's plan for marriage. The home should not be a battle zone but a place of refuge from the world.

The batterer who recognizes his sin of violence, repents of it, understands the triggers for his anger, and works to develop other ways to express himself will find new ways to grow in God's grace and strength. His recognition of God's intervention in his problem will strengthen his faith and his resolve to allow God to command his life. He can use this inward search to expose other areas in which God wants to work. Such an attitude change will open up new opportunities for him to use his God-given talents and gifts. He must determine to let God be Lord of his life and surrender the desire for control to the One to whom it really belongs.

This can be a long and difficult battle. That is why it is important, while he is in counseling, that a man have the support of other Christian men who can understand, *but will not tolerate or excuse,* his disposition toward violence. If your husband is not a Christian, but respects and likes some of the men in your church, perhaps he will allow them to help support his decision to seek help.

The Bible gives clear, concise responsibilities, rights, and privileges which are the focus of what God identifies as true manhood. Husbands have the responsibility to head their families in submission to the Lordship of Christ, a sacrificial attitude, and in God-given strength and wisdom. This leadership role requires that they be constantly aware of their own strengths and weaknesses. "Take heed unto thyself, and unto the doctrine; continue in them: for in doing this thou shalt both save thyself, and them that hear thee" (I Timothy 4:16).

A man who knows his own strengths has few problems in admitting his weaknesses. In areas where his strength falters, he can depend upon his wife, honestly and thankfully, to help carry the load. And he rejoices in using his strengths to encourage, and be encouraged by, her unique abilities (Proverbs 31:11,16). He supports, and is not threatened by, her intelligence and accomplishments. He does not need for her to assume an inferior position.

Marriage must be a shared effort by two adults. When either partner chooses to act like a child, refuses to grow to his or her potential, or expects to communicate needs and desires in inappropriate ways, the marriage is no longer a partnership. It becomes, instead, a bankrupt obligation.

Men have a right to live in godly freedom, but it is a freedom which does not condone the taking away of another's God-given rights. John 8:32, "the truth shall make you free," and other verses such as John 8:36, Romans 6:18-22, Ephesians 5:15,

Galatians 5:1, and I Peter 2:16 all define the scope and breadth of this godly freedom.

Like women, men also have the right of prayer, of communion with their Creator. "For there is one God, and one mediator between God and men, the man Christ Jesus" (I Timothy 2:5). James 5:16 highlights another facet of prayer: confession. "Confess your faults one to another, and pray one for another, that ye may be healed. The effectual fervent prayer of a righteous man availeth much." Men who have accepted Christ's work on the cross have the right to go boldly before the throne of God, expecting forgiveness and guidance (Hebrews 4:16).

Your Hope For the Future

Continue to pray for your spouse, your children, and yourself. Using the notes you have made in the previous chapters, review some of the abuse you have endured and God's grace which has sustained you. Pray specifically about these incidents; ask God to give you ways in which to escape the abuse. Pray that your spouse will be saved, if he is not a Christian, and that he will be shown how damaging his behavior is to each member of the family. Ask God to provide a counselor who can help your husband to reconcile his problems. Be willing to seek counseling for yourself.

Even though you may be exhausted by your burdens, never fail to offer prayers of adoration and praise to your heavenly Father. Be thankful that you have an omniscient God who cares about you. Thank God for who He is. Revel in His holiness. It will renew your perspective! This is not to suggest that a woman should praise God for an abusive husband. That would be tantamount to offering praise for sin. However, no matter how difficult your situation, God has provided you with blessings. Itemize these carefully, and be sure to offer thanks and praise for your children, your church, friends, good health, or a fruitful prayer life.

Ask God to increase your wisdom, multiply your faith, and strengthen your resolve not to be a doormat to another person. Ask for a godly wisdom of what it means to esteem others more highly than yourself (Philippians 2:3). Petition God for the gift of discernment which would help you to be less easily manipulated by false guilt and lies.

It is during prayer and Bible study that you should work through any feelings of sorrow toward the batterer. You may feel sad that he is afraid, feels alone or worthless. You can express this grief to God. Ask Him to help you avoid misusing this sadness or pity as an excuse for allowing him to continue being abusive. Pray for healing from bitterness and resentment, and that you will be able to forgive your husband for his behavior toward you. This forgiveness is not an acceptance of his abuse, but it is a decision to release the malice which you may feel. Then act upon that prayer. Act loving and forgiving even when you do not feel those emotions. Look for creative ways to express your forgiveness. And be sure to affirm to your husband the Source of your strength. Develop a godly dignity which refuses to accept abuse.

When you pray for your children, ask God to show you how you can increase their self-esteem and protect them from further harm. Ask specifically that you will be shown the gifts that each child has been given, and then encourage them to use these gifts. Pray for your children as individuals, offering thanks to God for each unique personality.

Try to take time each day to pray with your children. Often, they will express their fears and concerns when they pray. Help them to rely on God for comfort by showing them that you trust Him. Talk to your children. Don't try to deny or hide the situation. They're living it, too! Gently lead them to explore their feelings of pain, sadness or anger, and to ask God for protection and guidance. Give them positive, concrete steps to follow so that they can honor their father. Teach them that "in quietness and confidence" they can find strength (Isaiah 30:15). Give them ways to express their emotions. This might be in organized sports, music, drama, reading, hiking or biking. Above all, encourage them to spend time with their friends and help them to see other family structures where God is honored by the male leader in the home. Do not let them hide away, physically or emotionally, where they can let their negative emotions fester and become "bitter roots" (Hebrews 12:13-15). Encourage them to participate as fully as possible in the church programs for their age group(s). Then be sure you do, too.

In prayer, you will find the strength to support your children, to gradually forgive your husband, and the endurance to maintain your own balance.

FOOTNOTES

[1] Murray A. Straus, "A Sociological Perspective on the Prevention and Treatment of Wifebeating," in *Battered Women,* Maria Roy, New York, Van Nostrand Reinhold Co., 1977.

Evaluating Abuse in the Home

Which of the following statements apply to your husband?

___ He was abused by his parent(s) or saw his father abuse his mother.

___ He believes that women are inferior to men.

___ He can be charming, kind and loving, but often is surly or angry.

___ He believes that a man has a right to "discipline" his wife.

___ He is remorseful after an abusive incident, but soon begins to act abusively again.

___ He is sexually abusive.

___ He reacts with

   ___ verbal

   ___ physical

   ___ spiritual abuse when he is frustrated, stressed, disappointed or angry.

___ His abusive behavior is escalating, becoming more severe and/or more frequent.

___ He appears to have periods when it is difficult for him to distinguish between reality and fantasy.

___ He is defensive about his role as head of the family.

___ He claims that he cannot live without you or threatens to kill you rather than allow you to leave him.

___ He is involved in occult practices: witchcraft, spiritism, or other occult rituals.

___ He is extremely jealous or possessive.

___ He is abusive toward his children:

   ___ physically

   ___ emotionally

   ___ spiritually

___ He blames others for his problems.

1. List some areas in which you think your husband should share more responsibility. (i.e. child care, housework, financial support, spiritual leadership, etc.)

2. State some areas in which you think your husband tries to manipulate or control you, and list the behavior he uses to accomplish this. Use the lists of abusive behavior from chapters two, three and four.

Examples:

TYPE OF ABUSE	BEHAVIOR
A) controls financial matters	refuses to allow you to have the checkbook, and/or says you are incompetent with money
B) hampers your spiritual growth	makes fun of your faith and/or threatens to harm you if you go to church
C) intervenes in your social life	insults your friends and/or follows you if you go out
D) damages your self-image	calls you names, demeans your abilities, and/or blames you for provoking his abuse
E) manipulates your emotions	begs your forgiveness for his abuse, and/or promises it will never happen again, but refuses to seek a counselor and repeats the cycle

3. List some of the qualities which attracted you to your husband.

4. What are some of his qualities that you still admire or like?

List the best memories you have of your life with your husband.

5. What do you think are the most dangerous words or actions that your husband uses? Which cause the most damage to you or the children?

6. List the promises your husband made to you after his past abusive episodes that made you believe he would change his behavior. Mark with an X the promises which he has kept for more than one year.

7. List some of your spouse's inadequacies or failures for which he blames someone else. This list could include his parents, co-workers, employer, you, your children, law enforcement, the military, etc.

Examples:
  a) fired from his last job: blames his boss for being jealous of his abilities
  b) received a speeding ticket: blames the policeman for having faulty radar equipment
  c) his team lost the basketball game: blames the referees for being unfair

We all blame others in order to excuse ourselves at times. Study your list to see if your husband has a pattern of blaming others for his own actions or shortcomings.

8. List some of the Biblical characteristics of manhood. (See Proverbs 21:22-29, 22:1-12, 31:10-12; I Timothy 4:16; Ephesians 5:25-30; Philippians 2:3-8,14-15, 4:4-9; Galatians 5:16-23; Titus 2:7,8; II Timothy 2:15-25.)

9. Having reviewed some of God's qualities of proper manhood, what specific characteristics do you pray for in your husband?

10. What do you think are the most important changes for your husband to make in order to be a good husband and father?

Chapter 8
Childhood Of Fear: The Effects of Violent Behavior In Your Home

"Train up a child in the way he should go: and when he is old, he will not depart from it." (Proverbs 22:6)

Childhood should be a time of growth, of nurturing, and of building the foundations for a secure and self-respecting adult life. The family unit is his model for what is, and what can be. Too often, though, childhood memories reveal a family structure in which the child received a distorted and confusing view of himself; a view he carries into his future relationships.

From The Child's Point Of View

Children believe in absolute reality. Anything can be real. They must learn to doubt, to question, to disbelieve. They confuse fantasy with fact, misunderstand motives, and will accept as "normal" almost any situation they perceive as constant.

Children have no problem believing in God. They understand love; they desire protection. Moms and Dads are bigger than children, God is bigger than Moms and Dads. They believe in things they cannot see, hear, feel, taste, or smell. They have *faith*. For the first few years of their lives, they depend exclusively on their parents to provide food, shelter, clothing, and other tangible necessities. As their physical needs are met, their minds absorb the emotional and spiritual realities they perceive around them. To children, love is just as solid as a cookie, fear as real as a stomach ache, respect as concrete as a toy block. God and the angels are as near as their parents. They do not question or sift information they receive; they simply absorb it the way they understand it.

As they mature, children begin to question this *input* because they are expected to produce *output*. By the age of five, they have been laughed at, scolded, spanked, explained to, and molded. Their output is no longer a direct reflection of their perceptions. They have begun to inject doubt into what they think they see, use complicated filters to strain what they think they hear, and to think about consequences before they act. This is socialization. They are being trained to fit into the family, and later, into society.

Toilet training and table manners are part of a child's learned behavior. Desirable actions, reactions, and permissible demands for the child's age are part of what he learns to assess. *However, children often learn more by what we don't say, than by what we do say.* Attitudes and feelings are perceived with lightning speed, and often outweigh what the parent has communicated verbally. Contradictions between what children have been told and the reality of what they are shown are frightening and confusing to them.

Learning problem-solving techniques occupies a major part of a child's time. Physically, children are solving problems of balance, manual dexterity, and verbal expression. They learn to walk, to pick up small objects, to talk. Emotionally, they become more adept at finding acceptable outlets for feelings. They learn to share. They develop ways to protect themselves from emotional pain. Spiritually, they absorb what they are taught, and they begin to seek answers to questions. Because they are learning to question what is safe for them physically and emotionally, they start to move away from accepting what they perceive as absolute reality. They often begin to want more "proof" of God's existence.

As children grow, they piece together a puzzle. The parts sometimes seem fuzzy or upside down, but children will patch them together, painstakingly fitting one piece to another, until they have at least a partial picture they call "life." If violence in the home is part of the tiny picture on each piece, the children will complete a picture in which hitting, name-calling and disrespect are a focal point. Children look closely at these pictures. When they feel insecure, frightened, sad, or afraid, they use the coping skills displayed in the jigsaw. If they are told that these are not acceptable actions and attitudes, they become confused. If violence is a part of their lives, they often simply add a piece to the puzzle: I can't hit at school, at church, or at the park because someone will tell or hit me back. But, I can hit at home. Home is where it is okay to hit.

In The Middle

Children in violent homes often feel caught between their parents. The child need not see his mother beaten to know that there has been a fight. If children hear the sounds of a violent argument, they may huddle in their beds, or sometimes in the closet, afraid and alone. Many mothers have told me that their children have actually attacked the batterer in order to stop the fight. Children are frequently the ones who run to a neighbor or call the police during a violent episode. And sometimes they are punished for seeking outside help.

Children from families where violence is common are often secretive and withdrawn about their home lives. They seldom have friends over for more than a couple of hours, and avoid the times when their father is home or when their mother's bruises are obvious.

Older children will often stay outside or at a friend's house as much as possible to avoid being part of the confrontation. Others will hurry home from school as quickly as possible to help their mothers, trying to compensate for their father's abuse.

Some serious confrontations happen when a father begins to abuse the children. Women have taken beatings to protect a child the father wishes to "punish," succeeding in turning his anger away from the child at great suffering to themselves. Because of this, children sometimes believe that they are responsible for a parent's abusive behavior, identifying their own actions as being deserving of punishment. The child may feel guilty that mother got hurt protecting him. Soon the child has taken, emotionally, the full responsibility for the abuser's actions and for the mother's injuries.

Children sometimes become very protective of the batterer. They will lie to outsiders about his drinking or his violent behavior. They focus on how strong Dad is, or how smart, or successful. Seldom do children who have lived for long in a violent home express anything but admiration for their abusive parent to outsiders. They try desperately to reconcile the father they love with the abuser they hate. To protect themselves from this type of emotional turmoil, they pretend that "bad Daddy" doesn't exist, and that "good Daddy" is the only one they see.

Target Zones in Children

The physical abuse of children has received much needed attention in the media and the legislature. Children who were beaten previously, with no hope of outside interference, are now often helped by friends, neighbors, day-care workers, teachers. We all have a better idea what can be done to help the victims of child abuse and the help available to the parent(s) of that child. If you or your husband have been an abusive parent, there is help. Counselors, Social Service and Welfare Offices, schools, and churches all have access to information and referrals to help the abusive parent. Children understand when told that you have a problem, that sometimes you lose your temper, and that you want to learn to stop. Agencies try not to remove the child from the home if the abuse is relatively mild, or if the abusive parent begins counseling.

If the child is taken from the home, the parents can be given visitation rights if they are willing to learn how to stop the abusive behavior. Admitting that the abuse has occurred, and seeking help is the most important start toward a safe childhood for your child. If you are the abusive parent, seek help now. If your spouse has turned his battering on the children, you must protect them immediately. Call a child protection agency or the police, and report what you know has happened. Remove the child from danger, and inform your spouse that you have reported the child abuse and will not allow it to continue.

Most parents shudder at the thought of the sexual abuse of children. Yet, some women who live in abusive relationships discover that their children, most often daughters, are being or have been sexually abused by the batterer.

It is imperative that sexually abused children receive professional counseling as soon as possible. The mother who even suspects that such abuse is occurring or has occurred has an obligation to have the child checked by a doctor immediately or to be interviewed by a professional who is knowledgeable about incest.

If the danger of physical harm continues, you may have to leave your home. You may not discover the sexual abuse until after you do. The child may not have felt safe to reveal it. The batterer may have threatened her. She may not have felt that she would be believed.

Psychologist Fred H. Lindberg specializes in working with and counseling incest victims and their families. He has published studies in which he explores the traumatic effects of incest and serves as an expert witness in court cases involving incest. When asked to recommend a possible course of action for women who suspect that their children may have been victims of such an assault, he advised:

"The trauma of incest can often be greatly lessened by timely intervention. Should your child tell you about inappropriate touching or sexual overtures made by your husband, try to remain calm and encourage the child to tell you everything that has happened. You can lead the child gently, using words she is familiar with, to try to assess the situation.

"No matter how shocked or disgusted you may be by her

story, you must let her know that you believe her and that you intend to make sure it can never happen again.

"Children seldom lie about sexual abuse. A young child who relates knowledge about sexual activity with an adult is a victim. If she indicates that your spouse, whether or not he is her natural father, touched her inappropriately or forced her to touch him, she needs your immediate and unreserved understanding and help. In spite of how badly you may feel, make sure that you are able to support her and that you contact the proper authorities for help.

"It is rare for even an older child to falsely accuse a father or stepfather of sexual abuse. However, it is important that an investigation be undertaken which will rule out any likelihood of false accusations. Contact a local child protection agency, your family doctor, or a psychological services clinic and ask to be referred to someone who is experienced in treating sexually abused children. A competent child protection worker or psychologist will carefully question a child to insure that no manipulation of the facts exists. In the event that the child misrepresented the facts about the alleged sexual abuse, she and her family would be in a position to benefit from a professional psychological evaluation."

No mother wants to believe that her child has been abused. Or that her husband would do such a thing. However, it is dangerous to deny the possibility that your child has been victimized. Abusive behavior affects everyone in a family. Sexual abuse can be one aspect of that behavior. While it is understandable that a woman faced with evidence of incest would be shocked and confused, she must not waste time in denial. It is necessary for her to move quickly and effectively to protect her children from further harm. If you suspect that your children have been victims of sexual abuse, call your doctor, local child protection team at the Department of Public Assistance and Social Services (DPASS), or the police.

Children who are abused physically, including sexual abuse, develop problems with self-esteem. Children almost always assume that they deserve whatever happens to them. They will blame themselves more readily than they will accuse their parents.

Anxiety is a major problem for children of violent homes. They are afraid and worried because they cannot predict when or why the next blow-up might occur. They do not know what will trigger the next fight, but they try carefully not to be the cause. Children who live with violence fear the batterer. But, whether or not they have been abused, they begin to assume that the violence will always take place. They learn to live in fear, to function until the storm passes, to integrate the violence into their lives. They spend so much time coping with these issues that their emotional development may be hampered. Self-control, self-esteem, and normal non-violent reactions may be too much to ask of a child who must spend so much of his time simply surviving a violent environment.

The spiritual perceptions of children are easily confused. When Daddy batters, children often have trouble relating to a kind and loving God whom they are taught to call Father. Children can begin to believe that their mothers are punished by the abuser because God thinks they deserve it, or because God wills it. (If God made everything, why did he make my Daddy mad at my Mommy?) The child may perceive God as the villain in a plan to hurt him, his mother, or his father. (If God is supposed to take care of me, why did He let me get hurt?)

If your husband is spiritually abusive to you, it has a definite impact on the way your child relates to God. A father who refuses to allow Christian reading, storytelling, or teaching for his child lets the child know that he considers faith to be unimportant or even stupid. The Christian man who preaches against sin to his child, and then becomes violent, teaches the child that the Bible can be taken less than literally. The child who must hide the abuse in his family from church members enters a conspiracy of silence which can make him ashamed and reluctant to participate in fellowship.

The Future Seen Through the Past

Probable results of continued exposure to violent behavior are grim. Children from violent families tend to establish violent families. The problems of low self-esteem, lack of self-control, and the inability to escape the cycles run from generation to generation.

The batterer, in effect, writes a letter to his children. Instead of the blessing traditionally given to children by parents in the Old Testament, this birthright might read like this:

My Dear Daughter,
Throughout the years that you have lived in my home you have seen pain, humiliation, degradation, and fear. Now you are grown and will soon choose a mate. Because I have always shown that I was disappointed that you were not a boy, you know that you are not worthy of a man who would cherish you. Because I beat your mother, you know that a woman must be punished, must be controlled. Men cannot love without hitting, without hurting. You were born to be a victim. You, in turn, can neglect and abuse your children, striking out in pain and frustration. Live with the cycle of violence within your own home, but do not let the neighbors hear your cries.

or perhaps:

My Dear Son:
Now that you are a man, you must put aside the things of a child. Show no weaknesses, no fear, and blame your wife and children if you feel inadequate. Alcohol or drugs can mask some of your pain, and are a good excuse in case you go too far and injure someone. I never told you I loved you because I knew you'd have to be tough to be a man. I have carried the tradition of abuse from my own childhood. Act as I have acted, do as I have done, and continue to search for my approval, though it will probably never come. I am too miserable myself to offer you that gift.

These letters are dramatic examples of the worst kinds of abusive behavior. They are, in part, some of the messages that a child from an abusive family can receive.

If the abuse in your family is still less than all-out war, act now to protect your children, their futures, and yourself. You must assess what has happened to you and your children; look honestly at the already discernible effects of the abuse. Make a plan of action at the end of chapter nine and resolve to make both short-term and long-term changes.

If you perceive that the abuse is already at a dangerously high level, act now to remove your children from their home. Make an emergency plan of action and follow it at the earliest opportunity.

Assessing Your Child's Level of Abuse

Use the following statements to assess what abuse your children have endured. If you have more than one child, consider them individually, and use each child's initial to mark the statements which apply to them.

_____ Has your child been physically abused by you or your spouse?

_____ Has your child seen your spouse physically abuse you?

_____ Has your child been called "stupid" or other demeaning names by you or your spouse?

_____ Have you ever found bruises or other marks on your child after a time spent alone with his father which you suspect were caused by abuse? (Even if your child denies that he was abused.)

_____ Are you or your husband constantly critical of the child? Do you fail to praise him for his accomplishments and efforts?

____ Do you suspect that your husband has sexually abused the child in any manner?

____ Have you ever lied to a doctor, teacher or babysitter about an injury to your child caused by you or your husband?

____ Do either you or your husband complain about or demean each other to the child?

____ Has the child ever been told, by you or your husband, that God will not love him if he misbehaves?

____ Has your child ever been told, by you or your husband, that he is to blame for the anger and confusion in your home?

____ Has your husband told the child not to pray, or that he is not allowed to go to church?

____ Have you or your husband ever told the child that he was stupid or foolish when he asked a question, or wanted to share a song or story about Jesus?

Again, use each child's initial to mark the statements which apply.

____ Does your child repeatedly express physical abuse toward you or others?

____ Does the child appear to be withdrawn or depressed much of the time?

____ Has your child ever tried to protect you from your spouse, or begged you and his father to quit fighting?

____ Have teachers or other mothers repeatedly complained about your child's behavior?

____ Has your child been diagnosed by a doctor as hyperactive?

____ Does your child say that he thinks he is "stupid," "weird," or "ugly," or give other indications of low self-esteem, such as assuming he will fail at anything he attempts?

____ Does your child seem confused or upset by the different viewpoints you and your husband may express about God and the Bible?

____ Is your child unusually careful not to upset you or your husband for fear of extreme punishment?

____ Does your child refuse to discuss your husband's explosion of violence when you try to talk about it?

____ Has your child ever encouraged you to leave your husband because of abusive behavior?

____ Does your child avoid coming home or avoid bringing his friends home?

____ Does your child mimic your husband's abusive speech or actions, particularly toward you?

____ Does your child seem to approve of, or even to be proud of, your husband's drinking, use of force, or ability to frighten people?

____ Does he frequently question you about your decisions or actions, pointing out that "it might make Daddy mad"?

____ Do you know or suspect that your child uses illegal drugs or alcohol?

____ Does your child have repeated nightmares?

____ Does your child often complain of illnesses for which you can find no cause or medical explanation?

____ Does your child act very immature for his age?

____ Does your child often try to act like an adult, or try to take responsibilities beyond his capabilities?

____ Has a teacher, minister, or child-care worker told you that your child appears to have emotional problems?

Some of these statements are not particularly significant when taken alone. Many of these problems can be the result of a variety of disturbances in a child's life. Some are short-term problems which are easily resolved. Many of your answers will depend upon the age of the child. And, if you have more than one child, each may display different reactions. One may be boisterous and abusive, another may be withdrawn and depressed. A third child may not display any readily identifiable effects of a violent environment. But, if you begin to discern a pattern which indicates that domestic violence has been a contributing factor to your child's inappropriate behavior, it is time to seek outside help for yourself and your children even if your husband refuses to join you.

If your child repeatedly displays abusive behavior as a reflection of his home life, has been physically or emotionally battered by your spouse, has been the victim of sexual abuse by your spouse, or has witnessed repeated or severely abusive behavior, you should make plans as quickly as possible to leave your home and arrange to consult a counselor who is experienced in working with traumatized children.

If you have been abusive toward your child, put aside your own fears and shame and seek help immediately to insure that your child will be safe. The first step will be the most difficult to take. Once you have admitted your abusive behavior, you can find people who are ready and able to support your decision to change. You can benefit from counseling which will help you to develop proper parenting skills. The cycle of abuse can be broken—if you let it begin with you.

Chapter 9
Your Alternatives

"And I say unto you, Ask, and it shall be given you; seek, and ye shall find; knock, and it shall be opened unto you." (Luke 11:9)

There *are* alternatives to living in an abusive relationship. If you consider yourself to be cowardly, unable to take risks, think seriously about the jeopardy you are in every day. Living with a man who is abusive, even if it does not include physical abuse, puts you and your children at risk emotionally and spiritually.

Change is difficult. There will be times when it would be easier to remain in the patterns you have lived with for so long. The burden will sometimes seem more than you can bear. But the burden you now carry virtually insures that you will remain a victim. You can find the courage to change your life. Christ's promise to you is this: " . . . My grace is sufficient for thee: for My strength is made perfect in weakness . . . " (II Corinthians 12:9). When your determination weakens, read Joshua 1:9 and Isaiah 41:10-13, 43:1-7.

Rebuilding, Brick By Brick

If the abuse in your relationship is not frequent or severe, you may find many ways to strengthen the positive aspects of your marriage, choking out the seeds of abuse. Leaving an abusive spouse is a difficult, painful decision. But I encourage women to stay only when they have not experienced *any* severe abuse. If you have been brutalized physically, emotionally, or spiritually, and your husband is abusive much of the time, you must remove yourself from danger as soon as possible.

There are four concepts which are crucial to remaining in your relationship without accepting more abuse, or to your choice to leave in love. These are the building blocks of change for your life:

1) You have a right to decide that your safety is more important than his need to batter. You are worthy because you are God's child.

2) You can recognize abusive behavior and assess the potential dangers to your body, mind, and spirit.

3) You can choose to refuse his abuse, and to be willing to implement safe and effective plans to do so.

4) You need not accept physical, emotional, or spiritual abuse in the name of Biblical submission. Because your husband's abusive behavior is the ongoing willful commission of sin, you have the Scriptural right and responsibility to refuse to allow him to harm you.

"I have confidence in you through the Lord, that ye will be none otherwise minded: but he that troubleth you shall bear his judgment, whosoever he be" (Galatians 5:10).

Rating the Severity of Abuse

I will not attempt to decide for you if the abuse you endure is mild or severe, nor whether you should leave or stay. You now have the necessary information to help you honestly assess how the abuse is affecting you and/or your children. You should be ready to write out the plans of action as suggested later in this chapter.

1) At the end of chapters two, three and four, you marked the abusive actions, attitudes or words which you had experienced. Try to recall approximately how many times the abuse in each category has occurred:

____ physical ____ emotional ____ spiritual

115

2) How many damaging results of the abuse were you able to identify in yourself? _____

3) List those results which you consider to be the most damaging to you in each category.

physical   emotional   spiritual

4) At the end of chapter eight, how many examples of abuse did you believe one or more of your children has endured?
___ physical   ___ emotional   ___ spiritual

5) Approximately how many times has each type of abuse occurred?
___ physical   ___ emotional   ___ spiritual

6) How many damaging effects of the abuse have you been able to identify in one or more of your children?
child's name   effects

7) What do you consider to be the most damaging effects in each category? Put the child's name or initial beside the effects which each has shown.
___ physical _____
___ emotional _____
___ spiritual _____

8) I believe that it is physically, mentally, and/or emotionally:
___ not at all dangerous, ___ mildly dangerous,
___ moderately dangerous, ___ very dangerous
for me to remain with my husband because: _____

9) I believe that it is physically, mentally, and/or emotionally:
____ not at all dangerous,   ____ mildly dangerous,
____ moderately dangerous,   ____ very dangerous
for me to allow my children to remain with my husband,
because: _____
_____

A Decision to Stay

You may have decided that neither you nor your children are in enough danger physically, emotionally, or spiritually, to warrant leaving at this time. Even if you believe that there is some risk, you may be willing to accept that potential danger rather than to accept the financial, legal, emotional, or social consequences of separation.

You may never have worked outside the home. If you have few job skills, you may decide to stay until you have a better education or job training. Your decision may be based on the hope that you can safely delay leaving until your children are older. If you want to stay until you are better prepared to accept new responsibilities, beware of trading your safety, and that of your children, for the questionable security of your present situation.

If you have easily identified that your spouse's abusive behavior is cyclic, and if you checked several examples of abuse in any of the three categories, be careful to realistically assess how severe the problem is. Even a man who, at this point, has used only relatively mild physical abuse has the potential to seriously harm you the next time he explodes. And, it is unrealistic to think that frequent emotional and spiritual abuse alone cannot cause damage to you or your children.

You can use the following worksheet to help view the advantages and disadvantages of staying with your husband.

117

Advantages of Staying

Mark those which you think apply in your situation. Explore other possible advantages.

_____ I believe that staying will encourage my husband to seek God's forgiveness and change his behavior.

_____ financial security

_____ not having to work outside the home

_____ able to be with our children, not taking them to babysitter or daycare

_____ the times when my husband is loving, kind and caring; not abusive

_____ sharing friendships with other married couples

Disadvantages of Staying

_____ possible physical harm to me or the children

_____ continued damage to self-esteem or continued physical injury

_____ children growing up to believe violence is normal

_____ husband has total control over money

_____ limited chance to learn new skills because husband does not allow me to have a job or training

_____ not being able to go to church or see Christian friends

You will use this list of advantages and disadvantages when you complete your plans of action at the end of this chapter. Whether you choose to stay or leave, you may be able to lessen the disadvantages of the decision.

Having assessed the severity of the abuse, and being convinced that it is safe for you to stay, you can begin to take some steps for your own protection and comfort. Remember that if you choose to stay, _it need not be a permanent decision._ You can decide to leave any time you think the situation has worsened to an intolerable danger level.

Plan ahead for such an eventuality. Construct an emergency plan of action at the end of this chapter to be used should your spouse become increasingly abusive.

Find a minister or counselor to help you examine your situation. Complete the lists at the back of chapter ten to help you choose a counselor. These will help you know what to expect from a counselor and what your responsibilities will be. If you have trouble finding an individual who is knowledgeable about domestic violence, you can call or write the counseling centers listed at the end of the book.

Take time each day to pray for guidance and to give thankful praise for the rights, privileges, and responsibilities God has given you. Remind yourself that God has a plan for your life. In the face of name-calling, remember that your spouse need not have control over your feelings of self-worth. By completing the chart at the end of this chapter, you will examine some ways to help your children maintain their self-esteem.

Explore your talents. Review what you wrote down about your attributes and gifts at the end of chapter five. Try something different, like writing poetry, taking a class, or learning another language, just for fun. You may discover new talents. Don't automatically assume that you can't accomplish something until you have tried. Allow yourself the pleasure of new activities, even if you don't excel in them.

Implement your non-emergency plan of action from the end of this chapter. You can urge your spouse to seek help from a competent counselor. Confront his abusive behavior, alone or with your minister, if you believe it is safe to do so. Take advantage of any changes your husband makes which lessen his control over you. If he says that he will no longer object if you take a job, continue your education, or improve your relationships with friends and fellow Christians, use this new freedom. If he then becomes abusive because of reasonable choices you have made, you can confront his failure to keep his promise, or decide if you need to leave in order to protect yourself.

If your husband is willing to talk to you about his behavior without becoming abusive, you can begin to share the information about the cycle of violence. Encourage him to share his feelings in a non-abusive manner. Recognize and compliment his efforts toward change. Though you may find it easy to handle minor stress and frustrations without becoming angry or defensive, remember that he is just beginning to understand about the alternatives to abusive behavior. Ask him, or discuss together with a counselor, what types of encouragement and support are most helpful to him. He will probably find it easier to explore his behavior with a counselor rather than you.

Leaving In Love

Women who suffer severe or frequent abuse may find that a period of separation is necessary. The woman who endures physical battering (including pushing, shaking, or hitting) has no guarantee that her husband will not lose further control and put her in a life-threatening situation. Even if the abuse never becomes physical, a woman who perceives that she or her children have sustained even moderate emotional and spiritual damage would be wise to consider leaving before she feels unable to implement her plan. Because an abused woman becomes increasingly confused, isolated, and ego-battered, she sometimes waits too long. Too weakened by emotional abuse, she may find that she is unable to leave. And she runs the very real risk that her husband may suddenly begin to use violent physical force, even if he has never hit her before.

You may choose to leave during any phase of the cycle. As tension mounts, you would be wise to be ready to leave before your husband can hurt you. If you are caught unaware in the cycle, you may already have been injured and decide to leave on an emergency basis. It will be hardest for you to leave during phase three. It is during this phase that your husband has probably convinced you many times that he would never hurt you again. Though you may still want to believe him, you know that he will soon start phase one behavior again, and the cycle will repeat itself. You can believe that he means it when he expresses sorrow and guilt. But as his tension increases, his promises and his resolve to change will probably be forgotten.

If you view leaving as abandonment or desertion of your

spouse, examine your feelings carefully. It is possible to leave in love. You can love God and still want to protect the precious body, mind, and spirit that your husband would injure. You can love yourself, knowing that you were created for a divine purpose by the Father. You can love your children, working to give them an example which they can follow. Leaving can show love for your husband.

Even a man who agrees to counseling will return to his abusive behavior unless he has support to continue his alternative behavior, or *unless you are not there to abuse.* You can leave for a few hours or a few days in order to avoid further abuse. Though it may protect you from his immediate anger, leaving for a short period of time will probably not convince your husband that you will not accept further abuse.

The alternative to remaining with an abusive spouse is to leave indefinitely and to offer an ultimatum: either he gets help to stop his abusive behavior, or you will not return.

Inform your husband that you will tolerate no further abuse, *and mean it!* This is difficult counsel to give or accept because it goes against everything you have been taught about commitment, love, and loyalty. But it's crucial for your safety and your husband's future. Explain that his violence is cyclic, that you can recognize his phase of tension-building, and that you will not endure another violent episode. Recount to him the promises that he has already broken. In a calm and reasonable tone, tell him that you intend to take the children and leave the next time you observe that he is in phase one behavior. During the calm, loving phase, he may agree that it is best for you to leave. But, because he believes that he will not lose control again, he may not think you will have a plan which will enable you to escape. It is best to keep the details of your emergency plan to yourself so that he cannot interfere. Say nothing about your plan to leave or your perceptions of his cycle unless you can talk to him without putting yourself in further danger.

If you leave while he is gone, you may choose to leave a note which explains, briefly, that you have decided not to accept his behavior. You could state that you have gone to a safe place, and that you will arrange for someone to contact him as soon as possible with more information. Assure him that you have taken the children and that you are prepared to provide for their needs. You can then have your counselor, your minister, or a friend whom you trust not to reveal your whereabouts, call your husband to verify that you and the children are safe. This difficult step is actually the first one on the road to restoring your marriage.

Again, you may want to list the possible advantages and disadvantages of your decision.

Advantages of Leaving

____ affords greater protection from his abuse
____ may prove to my husband that I will not tolerate his behavior and may prompt him to seek help
____ can be an opportunity to make my own decisions
____ can give me time to help myself and my children recover from the abuse
____ can be an opportunity to break out of isolation

Disadvantages of Leaving

____ financial difficulties
____ loneliness
____ fear that my husband will come after me and harm me or the children
____ will have to leave my home and neighborhood
____ my husband may ask for a divorce

Constructing Your Plan

Recognizing problem areas is vitally important. Before you make either an emergency or a non-emergency plan of action, be sure you have pinpointed the abuse you and your children have endured in the relationship. This may seem cruel or petty, but it is a valuable tool. Consult the notes you made at the end of the previous chapters.

The exploration of past abuse has three important advantages for you. First, it allows you to face the actual actions and words which hurt you. By confronting these memories, you gradually take away their power to hurt you again. You can identify what you felt when the abuse occurred and what you feel now. You can see how the abuse progressed. Look for the cycles. Some are very regular; others are not noticeably predictable.

Explore the incidents of each type of abuse. Note if the abuse occurred when your spouse was drinking or using drugs. Where did the abuse occur? At home, in the car, at a friend's house? Were you alone with your husband, or were your children or other people around? Do you think that any of these factors contributed to the intensity of the abusive incident(s)? You may be able to see that certain situations or conditions contribute to the severity of the abuse. This will add to the store of information from which you must make your decisions.

Secondly, use the list to remind yourself how strong you are. This reflects the pain, humiliation, and degradation you have endured. But you are now able to say, "No more!"

Thirdly, use the list as a prayer guide. When you pray for your spouse, ask the Lord to help you forgive him for each word or action that hurt you. As you are able to turn loose of each incident, draw a line through it. This will not happen overnight. It is a process, a cleansing. If there are some items that you cannot forgive, explore them more deeply. Get in touch with the feelings which are still aroused by the memories. Do not feel guilty if you are unable to forgive him quickly. The wounds you have suffered are deep, but God is faithful. He will give you time and help to heal them.

Helping Our Children

Whether you stay or leave, you can take steps to help your children with their physical, emotional, and spiritual development. Whether or not your spouse is willing to join you in these efforts, you can begin to use some of these suggestions and add ideas of your own.

In chapter eight you assessed some of the abuses which your children have endured from your husband. With this worksheet, you can pinpoint any abusive behavior you may have used, and its possible effects. Using the list at the end of chapter eight, mark any statements which apply to your behavior toward your children.

1) Have you used: ____ physical
                   ____ emotional
                   ____ spiritual
abuse to control your children, or because you were angry and frustrated about your own victimization?

2) List the abuse which has been severe or frequent.

3) Which of these steps will you take to help you change your abusive behavior toward your children?
____ Confess your abusive behavior to the Lord, accept His forgiveness, and forgive yourself.
____ Ask the Lord to help you use proper non-abusive discipline, to encourage each child's self-esteem, and to provide a good example for your children.
____ Ask your counselor to help you with parenting skills.
____ Begin to find non-abusive outlets for your own feelings, and to learn ways to properly dissipate the immediate flash of anger.
____ Pinpoint what feelings trigger your abusive behavior. Then explore other possible choices: leave the room, put your child in his room or otherwise remove yourself from him before you become abusive.
____ Begin to be aware of daily opportunities to praise each child for his accomplishments, to support his efforts, and to encourage him to use his gifts.

____ If you have been severely abusive to your children, consider contacting Parents Anonymous or the local child protection authorities. Ask your counselor, your minister, or a trusted friend if they would help support you in this difficult decision. Admit honestly that you need and want help. Most parents can identify with how hard it is to balance proper discipline and nurture for their children. You will be amazed at how many people God will send to comfort and help you when you honor God by making a commitment to protect your children.

____ Other steps you might take: _____

4) Which of the following steps do you believe would encourage more open communication with your children? Your choices will depend on your childrens' ages, interests, and how your time can be structured.

a) Set aside time, perhaps fifteen minutes per day, to spend alone with each child. If possible, avoid interruptions like phone calls, other children, or household duties. Plan simple activities like singing a song your child chooses, coloring a picture, or encouraging the child to talk about concerns or interests. Make it a time in which you focus on the child as an individual. Avoid using the time to talk about any complaints or disciplinary problems you may have with the child.

b) Form a habit of praising the child more than you criticize him. Find several talents, accomplishments and characteristics in each child that you want to encourage. Though you must balance praise with appropriate discipline, try to insure that the child hears more about his achievements than he does about his mistakes. If you find that you have failed to balance praise and constructive criticism, don't feel guilty. Just take the child in your arms and love him. Don't be afraid to apologize if you have been wrong. Then remind yourself to look for, and express your pleasure about, positive qualities. When you must discipline, be sure to let the child know that his behavior may be inappropriate, but that you still think he is a good person. Tell your child that you love him every day.

c) Join your children for a bike ride, a game of tag, tennis, or a walk in the park. Young children who have enjoyed hard physical exercise are less likely to be rambunctious at home. Older children often balk at your suggestions, but enjoy the outing if you let them choose a reasonable activity.

d) Refrain from using labels or unkind names for your child. Whether you use them either in an attempt at humor or in frustration, calling a child "shorty" or "stupid" can wear away at his self-esteem.

Other ideas you may want to implement: _____

---

5) List some of the ways you can help your children know and love God. Modify the plans if you live with a husband who is likely to become abusive if you act on these suggestions. Also, consider the ages and abilities of your children.

a) Tell the children what God does for you. Relate specific answers to prayer. Share some of the insights you receive from God in difficult situations. Be a faithful witness to your children.

b) Pray with your children every day. Encourage them to pray aloud to express their praise and their needs.

c) Read Bible stories, or discuss men and women whom God used in special ways.

d) Be willing to apologize to your children if you hurt their feelings, say something mean in anger, or are unfair to them. Tell them that you have asked God's forgiveness, and that you would like them to forgive you for your mistake. Lead them by example in learning to recognize their offenses and in asking for forgiveness from God and others.

Other ideas you may want to implement: _____

Gathering Information For Your Plans

Whether you decide to stay or to leave, you should develop both emergency and non-emergency plans of action. Your emergency plan must be relatively simple and easy to follow. You will find a worksheet in this chapter which will help you form a realistic, workable emergency plan. Review this plan occasionally whether you plan to stay with your husband or to separate in the future.

Your non-emergency plan can have both short- and long-term goals and ideas. You will find examples of non-emergency plans for women who remain with their husbands in this chapter. The worksheet for those who choose to separate can be completed better after reading the information in chapter ten and is contained in that chapter. Both worksheets contain information which will be important in each situation/decision.

First, you must gather some information. Call a minister who counsels battered women or a domestic violence agency. Ask them to help you explore your options. Whether you stay with your spouse or leave, your emergency plan demands that you weigh the advantages and disadvantages of safe places to go, specify the transportation you may use, and determine the availability of resources.

When Will You Leave?

Decide whether you will leave when your husband begins to become anxious or tense, or whether you will wait until you feel that an explosion is imminent. You cannot control or predict your husband's behavior, but you can be aware of his demeanor. Watch for signs of increasing tension, critical attitudes, and/or an increase in drug or alcohol use. If he seems to be cycling toward a fight, you may be able to make an excuse to leave. Tell him you need to go out if it is not likely to make him angrier. If you must, wait until he is in another part of the house before you leave or call the police to escort you out.

If your husband has never become physically violent, you could be surprised by an unexpected physical attack. If he does explode, you may be injured but not incapacitated. He may go to sleep or leave the house after becoming violent. If you can, quietly take the children and leave. This is a positive step to take. Do not give him excuses even for a "first" time. Show him that you do not choose to accept that kind of behavior, and you will not allow yourself or your children to be harmed.

Consider the opportunities to escape you have available in an emergency and be prepared to go. There are women who have taken their children and run from their homes, barefooted and pajama-clad, at three o'clock in the morning. They were terrified and confused. But they are alive. By planning ahead, you may be able to avoid this kind of desperate emergency.

How Will You Leave?

Think about what kind of transportation you will use if you leave. If you have a car, keep extra keys in a place where you can reach them quickly. Have an alternate plan for transportation, if you are unable to take your car. Do you have a friend who has offered to drive you to a chosen place of safety? Could you take a cab? How far would you have to walk to reach a phone? Consider all your alternatives. Ask people who know about your situation if they would be willing to help. Try to determine the safest way for you to escape with your children.

Where Will You Go?

Your family, friends, church, or a secular agency may be able to give you a safe place to go in an emergency.

Talk to your minister or call a Christian counseling center to find out if there is a church which operates a shelter or safehouse should you need to leave your home.

Look in the phone book under Women's Resources, Family Violence, Domestic Violence, Crisis Intervention, or Community Help Programs to see if your town has a secular domestic violence agency. Call the local police station and ask if they know of such an agency.

Consider the advantages and disadvantages of any place you have chosen. Think carefully about its availability, confidentiality, and security. When you decide which place is the best for you, be sure you know its exact location and that you can reach it quickly when you are upset or when it is dark. If your choice is a shelter, call and get specific instructions as to how you will be admitted. Ask them if they are able to provide transportation to the shelter.

Can you arrange to have enough money or a credit card you can use to pay for one night in a motel? If so, decide which motel you will use, and make sure you can find it easily in an emergency.

What Will You Take?

The less you have to take with you, the faster you will be able to leave. Decide which items are necessary, and where you can keep them in order to be able to get them, and get out, quickly.

____ clothes for you and the children
____ car keys and house keys
____ a toy or blanket which is important to your child
____ emergency money: saved from your paycheck, saved from household expenses, or borrowed from a friend or relative
____ checkbook, credit cards
____ any special medication you or a child may need
____ originals or copies of important documents or papers:
    ____ your driver's license or other identification
    ____ a green card or citizenship papers if you are a legal alien or a new citizen
    ____ birth certificates for you and the children
____ phone numbers of your minister, friends, counselor or domestic violence agency
____ a list of joint bank accounts, loans, or credit cards and their numbers
____ other items: _____

Do you have a cupboard, closet or drawer in which you can safely store these things? Could you keep them in the trunk of your car, hide them in the garage, or leave them at a friend or neighbor's home?

Other storage places _____

Decide what calls you need to make to implement your emergency plan. Write down the information you receive during these calls and use it to make your plan more safe and effective.

If you need different or additional information for a non-emergency plan of action, make those calls, too, and incorporate the information into your plan. Decide to make the calls for your emergency plan at the earliest opportunity. The calls for your non-emergency plan can be made over the next week or two. Avoid planning to do it "soon," or worse, "someday."

Questions or Concerns	Person	Phone Number
Available safehouse or shelter	minister counselor domestic vio- lence agency	_____ _____ _____
police procedure for family violence calls; possible transportation to shelter; information about agencies which help victims	local police or sheriff's office	_____
your financial and legal rights and responsibilities under the law; child custody; division of property; legal separation	Legal Aid Office lawyer county court- house	_____ _____ _____
transportation or other help in an emergency; (support, financial assistance, a place to store emergency supplies or valuable items, ability to care for a pet)	friend relative neighbor	_____ _____ _____
school attendance or daycare for your children; protecting children from your husband; transportation for children	school district office school principal child's teacher daycare provider	_____ _____ _____ _____

130

Emergency Plan of Action

When will you leave? _____

What transportation is available to you? _____
_____

Where will you go? _____

What will you take? _____
_____

Where will you keep these items? _____

Who may be able to help you leave, or help you once you
have left? _____

Non-emergency Plan of Action—If You Stay

The woman who chooses to remain with her husband will
need a non-emergency plan which will provide both short- and
long-term ways to improve her life and marriage.

1) Write down your reasons for staying.

2) If it is safe for you to confront your husband about his
abusive behavior, plan the key points of what you want to
say.

3) Will you confront him alone or with support? Who might you consult for advice, or ask to help you talk with your husband?

4) When will you implement this plan?

5) How can you best encourage and support your husband if he chooses to seek help?

6) What physical activities will you use to increase fitness and to relieve stress?

7) When will you begin these activities?

8) What steps will you take to protect and/or increase your self-esteem?

9) When will you begin?

10) What spiritual goals do you have as a Christian? How can you begin to work toward those goals? Consider your God-given privileges, rights and responsibilities. Be specific in naming your goals. (Examples: Responsibility to treat my body as God's temple: I will eat nutritious meals. Right to pray: I will pray specifically for any unsaved members of my family daily. Privilege of being a good teacher: I will offer to help teach a Sunday School class.)

11) When will you begin to take these steps?

12) Name some personal goals for your life: making a new friend, acquiring new skills, furthering your education, seeking employment, etc. Again, be specific about what you would like to achieve and when. Give yourself a time schedule.

13) What arrangements do you need to make in order to achieve these goals? (Child care, signing up for a class, checking help wanted ads, writing a resume, etc.)

14) When will you begin to make these arrangements?

15) Complete the following sentences:
I am _____
I can _____
I feel _____
I think _____
I want _____
Five years from today, _____

Review these statements frequently to help you keep in touch with yourself. In addition to this plan, review and act on a plan to help your children.

Chapter 10
Information For The Woman
Who Separates

"Restore unto me the joy of thy salvation; and uphold me with thy free spirit." (Psalm 51:12)

Your legal, financial, emotional, and social needs will change the moment you decide to separate from your husband. Being prepared for such change will ease this difficult transition. Gather information in these areas for both your emergency and non-emergency plans of action.

Some of your minor legal questions can be answered by a counselor well-versed in domestic violence. You can call legal aid, a lawyer, or the county courthouse to find out about custody rights, restraining orders, family violence protection orders, or your legal and financial responsibilities while you are separated. Many domestic violence organizations provide advocates who will accompany you to court or to meet with Welfare, children's services, or a lawyer. Take advantage of this support.

Though you can leave your husband without filing for a legal separation, it may need to be one of your considerations. It has advantages over simply leaving because child custody and individual financial responsibilities can be clearly outlined. The lawyer's fees vary depending upon the complexity of the document and can be as high as those involved in filing for divorce. When you have had time to collect your thoughts and to prepare yourself for a discussion with him, contact your husband by phone or letter. Ask him if he would be willing to consider a legal separation. If you assure him that you do not want a divorce because you believe that your marriage can be healed, and that you would like to work with him toward the healing, perhaps he will agree to this alternative.

If possible, take your children with you when you leave your home. The court will probably award at least temporary custody to the parent who has the children with him or her when a dispute arises. And, even if your husband has never been violent toward them, he may strike out in anger when he finds you gone.

If law enforcement officers are with you when you leave, or if your husband is not there, you may take a few extra minutes to collect some of your more valued possessions and important documents. (See the list at the end of this chapter.) Often, a husband will destroy a wife's belongings when he finds that she has left. If you have planned in advance to leave, you can transfer these to a friend's home or another safe place. If you must implement your emergency plan, you should have these documents in a convenient place. If you can, make arrangements to have a friend, relative or animal clinic care for your pet, but do not jeopardize your safety to protect an animal.

Many men try to control their wives by keeping them financially dependent. Half of any assets you and your husband have in a joint checking or savings account are yours to take, unless the law in your state specifies differently. You may need to remove this money as soon as possible. Your husband could freeze these accounts and keep you from having access to them. Do not feel guilty for taking what is rightfully yours.

Emotionally, you may find yourself at a very low point. If you are confused or feel as if the problems will never improve, re-read the chapter on spiritual realignment. Consult your lists about the abusive behavior you have endured, and pray for strength, for guidance, for peace.

As you search the Bible, think of positive ways to implement God's promises in your life. Be creative!

"That he would grant unto us, that we being delivered out of the hand of our enemies might serve Him without fear, . . . To give light to them that sit in darkness and in the shadow of death, to guide our feet into the way of peace" (Luke 1:74,79).

Lean on God, and reach out to people eager to provide help. God will help them to share your burden. They, too, will grow through your willingness to share.

"Bear ye one another's burdens, and so fulfill the law of Christ" (Galatians 6:2).

Recognize what feelings are negative or damaging for you at this point and confront them in yourself. Find Scriptures that answer your concerns and support the good feelings you have. Copy or mark the most helpful ones and read them often. Use a concordance to help you find verses. Your Bible may have a small concordance in the back. Look under "hope," "fear," "freedom," "confusion," "blessings," "tears," and "wisdom." Allow yourself time and privacy in order to explore what you feel. (See Mark 6:30,31.)

As you sift through your feelings in private, before our holy God, consider what He can help you learn during this time.

"Therefore being justified by faith, we have peace with God through our Lord Jesus Christ: By whom also we have access by faith into this grace wherein we stand, and rejoice in hope of the glory of God. And not only so, but we glory in tribulations also: knowing that tribulation worketh patience; and patience, experience; and experience, hope. And hope maketh not ashamed; because the love of God is shed abroad in our hearts by the Holy Ghost which is given unto us" (Romans 5:1-5).

"And we know that all things work together for good to them that love God, to them who are the called according to his purpose. For whom he did foreknow, he also did predestinate to be conformed to the image of his Son . . . . If God be for us, who can be against us?" (Romans 8:28-29,31).

Weigh the advantages of the safe places available to you, particularly if you feel it necessary to remain separated for an indefinite period of time. The private home of family or friends has the advantage of allowing you to be with people you know and trust. Your children may be less frightened in a home with familiar people. But if your husband tries to come after you, the people you are with could be in jeopardy as well. Also, if the people do not understand the issue of domestic violence, they may be easily manipulated by your husband into believing that the problem can be quickly solved and that you should return to him immediately.

There is a safehouse system used in some cities. These are usually people who volunteer their homes to provide temporary shelter for women in need of help. You and your children will probably have your own bedroom, and perhaps share a bath with the family. One of the advantages is that the location of the safehouse is almost surely unknown to your husband. Some disadvantages may be that the safehouse could be crowded, you may have little privacy, or you may feel that you are imposing upon the family.

Shelters for battered women are becoming more common in every state. A shelter is a home or other building run by an organization which provides protection and counseling specifically for battered women and their children. The way in which these shelters are managed differs in each community. Most provide information and referrals to other needed agencies such as Welfare, DPASS, and Legal Aid. One of the advantages of a shelter is its security and confidentiality. Many have elaborate alarm systems, often linked to the local police department, making it difficult for an angry husband to gain access. The disadvantages may include being in an unfamiliar place, or explaining to young children the need to keep the shelter location secret.

If you have school-aged children, a domestic violence agency can give you some guidelines on arranging for them to continue to attend their classes. Call the school or the district office to find the best solutions. If you have a car or can arrange transportation, you could allow your children to continue at their present school. However, if your husband is likely to harass the children at school, or if you think he might kidnap them, you may have to consider changing schools for their protection. In either case, discuss the situation with the teachers so that they can help the children through this transition and alert you to any problems. Ask them specifically to call you if they notice that your child seems unhappy, withdrawn, anxious, or rebellious. Let the principal know if you have a restraining order or other document which restricts the times or conditions under which your husband has visitation. If so, the school can refuse to allow him access to the children during school hours.

You may have to depend on friends, family, your church, or public assistance for your financial needs. Remember that there is no shame in accepting help. Look on this time as one in which you can begin to order your priorities. Your safety and that of your children is of prime importance.

If you have never had a social life, begin to make friends by offering your friendship to others. You can have lunch with a woman acquaintance at work instead of eating alone. If you already belong to a church, a club, or another organization, continue to attend. But be aware that when you are at your usual meetings or services, your husband has access to you. Be cautious and use sound judgment if you think he is looking for you or could still be dangerous.

Explain to those who inquire, if you wish, that you and your husband have separated. Whether you give any details of your problem is your choice. Be willing to accept the concern of friends, family, and church members without telling them more than you want them to know. True concern will focus on how the person can help you and will be given in the spirit of love. Prying questions, bad advice, or reprimands can be put aside if you consider how many people are truly ignorant concerning the issues of domestic violence. You have enough strength to be secure in your belief that you are doing the right thing.

Unfortunately, your pastor and other people in your church may present a confused or even disapproving attitude. Many truly believe that a woman is never right in leaving her husband. Some will be unaware of the abuse you have endured, and of how difficult it was for you to make the decision to leave. They have not walked your path. They cannot reach inside you and feel what you feel. Remember that it is possible for people be to loving, kind, and committed Christians, and still carry unreasonable prejudices and beliefs. Inexperience and narrow-mindedness often walk hand in hand. Perhaps a woman who openly disapproves of your separation is herself a victim who has martyred herself to her husband's abuse. She may believe that no matter how bad her own relationship becomes, she must stay rather than accept responsibility for her own safety. Try to be gentle with these people, but do not allow them to intrude upon your newfound feelings of self-esteem.

Communicating Safely With the Batterer

If you did not have time to leave a note explaining your sudden absence, you can have your counselor help you take steps to let your husband know you are in a safe place, but that you are not prepared to give its location. During this conversation, have the counselor assure your husband that you and the children are all right. If you do not believe that he would harm the children, or bully them into disclosing where you are staying, arrange for him to see them at a safe location. Perhaps your minister or a friend would be willing to take them to him for a few hours and then pick them up. Emphasize to the children that they must not tell their father where you are staying. Reassure them that their father loves them, but that you must remain separated for a while. Write a letter, have a friend or your counselor call him, but do not personally contact him at this time. You are extremely vulnerable to his phase three behavior. Do not allow yourself to be persuaded to return to him unless you have had time to settle yourself and sort through your emotional chaos. This is the time to work closely with a counselor who can help you make informed decisions.

Choose carefully those with whom you discuss your problem. Friends and family mean well, but they are often easily manipulated by the abuser. You know from your own experience how easy it is to feel sorry for him when he is in phase three behavior. A friend or family member who sees your husband as a broken, sorrowful man who desperately wants to rebuild his marriage is likely to give him information about where you are staying, working, or how to reach you by phone. Because you need this time to begin to heal and to explore your position, you may not want to contact him at all. It may be enough at this time to just let him know you are safe. A domestic violence counselor can help you to do that without putting yourself in jeopardy.

If you remain separated from your husband for several weeks, you may decide to rent an apartment or house for you and your children. After leaving the security of a friend's home or a shelter, limit your contact with the batterer in order to protect yourself. If you have a restraining order that restricts your husband from attempting to contact you, keep a list of when and where he tries to call or see you. If you must, report him to the police so that they can enforce the order.

Gradually, you can allow your husband to call you, or you can call him at arranged times. Be adamant in your stand that these conversations will terminate immediately if your husband becomes abusive or manipulative. If he yells at you, calls you names, threatens you, or demeans you, simply tell him that you will not accept his abuse, and hang up. Don't argue with him, or stay on the phone hoping to hear words which will convince you that it is safe for you to return to him. You need to see action on his part. Going to a counselor and working to find non-violent ways to cope are the things which will help him to change his behavior.

You can prepare yourself for some of his manipulative techniques by reviewing the list of phase three behaviors which you described at the end of chapter seven. If they worked once to convince you to stay, he will probably try them again. Be aware that he will try to make you feel guilty. Many batterers complain that they haven't eaten in days, that they have no clean clothes, or that the house is a mess. Remind yourself that he is an adult who is capable of caring for himself. He can (and should) learn to cook, do laundry, and clean the house. He may drop vague hints that he intends to harm himself. Tell him that you are concerned, and that you would be glad to call your minister or one of his friends to talk to him. If he refuses their help, there is little you can do without endangering yourself. He will probably blame you for upsetting the family and accuse you of not caring about him or the children. You can remain calm and refuse to accept his manipulations if you remind yourself:

1) He chooses to use abusive behavior.

2) He made it unsafe for you to remain with him because of his behavior.

3) He can make the choice to go for help. If he wants the family restored, he will take that responsibility.

If your husband has sought help, and you believe that he has changed his behavior enough to allow you to begin to see him without fear, ask a counselor or knowledgeable friend to help you make a list of meeting places where you will be safe. Perhaps you can meet on neutral ground, such as your pastor's office or at the domestic violence agency. You may have allowed him to visit the children at a friend's home or to keep them for a weekend if you did not think he would harm them. Now you could begin to join your husband in taking your children roller skating, to the park, or to church. Meet your husband in a safe place both alone and with your children to re-establish your relationship.

Be very careful not to let your loneliness or pity for your husband be your prime reason for returning to live with him before he has fully explored and altered his behavior patterns. Many women leave their husbands and return after only a few weeks because they have seen their husbands make progress in avoiding abusive behavior. However, it usually takes months for a person to make lasting changes in behavioral patterns. Women who have lived in abusive relationships need time to heal and to develop appropriately assertive and reasonably self-protective ways in which to live. When wives return before their husbands have fully integrated their abilities to use non-violent coping skills, it is likely that they will see their husbands begin a gradual, or perhaps dangerously sudden, return to the old abusive patterns.

If your husband has worked with a counselor or pastor, and/or has regularly attended a support group for batterers, ask him to share some of what he has learned. Go slowly. Allow him to express his feelings and face his own actions without accusations or reminders from you. Whatever time is required for each of you to heal and to process the changes is worth it.

In separating, you have made a strong statement to your husband and to yourself. You have decided that you are not going to be a victim again and that your husband must make the choice to change his behavior. Do not accept any compromise on the subject of abuse. Your husband may decide that it is too painful for him to accept that he needs help. He may give you an ultimatum: return to the marriage, or he will file for divorce. If you are truly committed to remaining married to him, hopeful that he will change, the threat of divorce may be devastating to you. The turmoil that you will feel is natural. Your first inclination may be to return in order to avoid losing him. The resolve you once felt—the strong conviction to leave in love—seems gone. You may think that you made the wrong decision, and feel confused as to whether leaving was your best option. You will probably feel guilty, thinking that you forced him to ask for a divorce. In reality, the threat to divorce you is only another way for him to control you, to manipulate you into bending to his will. If he follows through, he has chosen to lose his family rather than face his problem and to change.

Divorce

Divorce may be an automatic response to problems in a marriage where neither partner is concerned about God's Word. To a Christian spouse, though, divorce involves the dissolution of a bond to which he or she attaches more than legal value. Divorce, and its consequences, abound in social myths. The myths are compounded by our society's continuing devaluation of the family.

142

One myth that society encourages is that divorce provides freedom. The depth of commitment a spouse has to the marriage vows can depend upon what expectations he or she has carried into the marriage. On one hand, there are men and women who divorce without serious attempts at reconciliation because of "irreconcilable differences." Often, this simply means that one or both partners refuse to take responsibility for themselves and for the relationship. In divorcing, these people have not attained freedom. Often, they simply exchange one set of problems for another. On the other hand, I have seen men and women who tolerate adultery, beatings, and total irresponsibility on the part of their spouses, but will not entertain the idea of a separation, let alone a divorce. These people are sometimes so caught up in being self-righteous sufferers that they allow themselves, and their children, to be slaves to the errant partner's will.

Society has glamorized divorce. Most divorced people will tell you that the process is very painful, filled with guilt and uncertainty. Television and movies have only recently begun to portray some of the agonizing results of divorce: children who are bounced between two separate families; women who juggle a job and single parenting, and men who are part-time fathers.

Another misconception is that all family members will automatically be happier because of the divorce. The spouses and children sometimes never communicate their fear, insecurity, or confusion over the divorce. The husband and/or wife may be too caught up in anger and the desire to strike back. Any or all family members can be more miserable than they were before the divorce. Divorce is never a magical solution to problems, though it may be the option a spouse must consider.

Divorce is a highly controversial issue in Christian churches. Some churches believe that divorce is totally forbidden by the Bible. They will not counsel for divorce under any circumstance, though they may admit the need for separation. Others consider divorce a solution if no other alternatives seem possible. Both liberal and conservative churches can cite

Scriptures which they believe uphold their viewpoints. As a Christian woman, you may be confused as to what the Scriptures say concerning the dissolution of a marriage.

I will not make a recommendation one way or the other. It is a very painful, personal decision. Instead let me simply point out the verses in which God deals with this subject.

The Scriptures do speak of divorce and of remarriage. Deuteronomy 24:1-4 is the beginning of the laws which Moses was instructed to give the Jews concerning divorce. Ezra 9 and 10, and Malachi 2 both deal with attitudes and conditions for divorce. In the New Testament, Jesus speaks of divorce in Matthew 5:32 and 19:9, Mark 10:1-12 and Luke 16:18. First Corinthians 7:10-16, 27-28 and verse 39 will give you still more information.

I have not attempted to interpret these Scriptures. Carefully read each reference, asking for help from the pastor of your church, or from a friend whose Biblical knowledge you trust. Remember that in reading these verses, their context and place in Scripture are vitally important. Consider their meaning in light of what you know to be God's will in your life. As you read, you will be able to use other Scriptures to properly reconcile your interpretations of Christ's teachings on divorce. Explore God's Word in prayer and willingness to listen.

The primary purpose of this book has been to provide information for women in abusive situations and to help the reader to be aware that there are alternatives to living in a violent home. Divorce is one of the alternatives. I cannot suppose to know what God will direct you to do. You may choose divorce in order to escape a man who refuses to change his behavior, or he may choose to divorce you rather than seek help toward healing the marriage. Search the Scriptures in light of your particular situation. I have tried to help you to order your physical, emotional, and spiritual selves so that you can freely explore what your Father has planned for you.

During your separation, spend time in prayerful consideration of the changes which must occur in order for your marriage to be rebuilt. Review what you like about your husband, what qualities you admire, and what changes he must make to allow you to return to him safely. Give him time in which to change his behavioral patterns permanently. Encourage his efforts.

If your spouse refuses to implement necessary changes, you can begin to make decisions about how you will proceed. You may decide to remain separated indefinitely. However, if you and/or your spouse ultimately choose to divorce, you should be cautious about rebounding into another relationship. There is a very real danger that you could choose another abusive man if you have not analyzed your victimization. Many women have had several disastrous marriages because they are convinced that they must have a romantic relationship in order to avoid loneliness or to feel complete as a woman.

These attitudes should be explored. If you think that you *need* to be married, you may still view yourself as a possession, or consider yourself helpless without a husband to protect you. Marriage is not an automatic defense against loneliness. Men and women can be complete, fulfilled people regardless of their marital state. Put into effect some of the concepts and activities you have developed which allow you to protect and enhance your life. Then you will be able to make an informed decision about possible future relationships. Above all, give yourself—and God—time.

Taking A Stand

In the previous chapter you had the opportunity to assess the danger level of your relationship. If you have chosen to separate, you should complete both the emergency plan of action in chapter nine, and the non-emergency plan of action at the end of this chapter. Using these worksheets as guides, you can make lists for almost any area in which you need to order your thoughts and feelings. It is constructive to list your alternatives, and it may help you to understand what considerations relate to your particular situation.

Keep these lists in a safe place where your spouse or children will not have access to them. You are entitled to the privacy of your thoughts. Refer to your lists when you feel confused, lonely, manipulated, or unsure of your decisions. They can be a vital part of staying connected to the reality of your situation and ease any feelings of helplessness.

Non-emergency Plan of Action—If You Separate

The woman who plans to separate from her husband will need non-emergency plans to be used while she is not in immediate danger. These should provide her a safe place to go and a way to begin to rebuild her relationship.

1) Write down your reasons for separating.

2) When do you plan to leave?

3) How long do you intend to stay separated?

4) Under what conditions would you return?

5) When you leave your husband, where will you go? Refer to the information gathering worksheets.

6) What will you take with you?

7) What plans, if any, have you made to store those possessions which you want to take but cannot move immediately to your safe place? Do you have someone to care for any pets?

8) What transportation will you use to get to your safe place?

9) Write down any specific questions or concerns you would like to discuss with your husband. (Legal separation, financial obligations, child visitation, etc.)

10) What will you do before contacting your husband personally? (Pray for healing and for strength; pray that he will be receptive to God's Word; be aware of husband's manipulative techniques; allow time to prepare notes on confronting him in love.)

11) Will you confront him in a letter, on the phone, or in person? Will you confront him alone or with support?

12) Who might you consult for advice, or ask to help you talk to your husband?

13) When will you implement this plan?

14) How can you best encourage and support your husband if he chooses to seek help?

15) If you are in physical danger from your spouse, what steps will you take to protect yourself and your children? (Legal restraining or protection orders, keeping your location secret, having law enforcement phone numbers handy, going to a safe place in another town, etc.)

16) What physical activities will you use to increase fitness and to relieve stress? When will you begin?

17) What steps will you take to protect and/or increase your self-esteem? When will you begin?

18) What spiritual goals do you have as a Christian? How can you begin to work toward those goals? Consider your God-given privileges, rights, and responsibilities. Be specific in naming your goals. (Examples: I will eat nutritious meals. I will pray specifically for unsaved members of my family daily. I will offer to help teach a Sunday School class.)

19) When will you begin?

20) Name some personal goals for your life: making a new friend, acquiring new skills, furthering your education, seeking employment, etc. Again, be specific about what you would like to achieve.

21) What arrangements do you need to make in order to begin? (Child care, signing up for a class, checking help wanted ads, writing a resume, etc.)

22) When will you begin to make these arrangements?

23) Complete the following sentences:
I am _____
I feel _____
I think _____
I want _____
Five years from today, _____
Notes: _____

Review and update these statements frequently to help you keep in touch with yourself. In addition to this plan, review and act on the plan you made to help your children.

Chapter 11
Choosing A Counselor

" . . . Add to your faith virtue; and to virtue knowledge; and to knowledge temperance; and to temperance patience; and to patience godliness." (II Peter 1:5-6)

Christian women in abusive relationships have special needs for a counselor well-versed in domestic violence, and attuned to their unique needs for Biblical principles and reassurances.

A counselor is not a psychiatrist or a therapist. Rather, a counselor is a trusted confidante, a helper. But a counselor can only help a person to explore her own situations, feelings, goals, and attitudes. He/she is not able to make decisions for you, but should provide you with information and list some possible solutions from which you may choose.

It is possible that you will prefer to work with a woman. Some women feel more comfortable or find that another woman can emphathize with their victimization. Others believe it is valuable to work with a man in order to obtain a masculine viewpoint. I have found that support and empathy can be a part of counseling from both men and women. Women who have been victimized by a man may find a female counselor less likely to engender further feelings of inferiority. And, it is often easier to tell a woman personal details concerning humiliation, degradation, or specific sexual acts and attitudes. Consider your emotional state and choose a counselor with whom you are comfortable and whose abilities you trust.

The Christian Counselor

Many Christian women are more comfortable dealing with a counselor who shares their Christian viewpoint. In assessing the counselor's ability to help you, explore his/her church affiliation, experience in working with domestic violence victims and batterers, and his/her ability to offer proper support and confidentiality in counseling with you.

If you want a Christian counselor, feel free to ask questions about his/her beliefs. If your church has a counselor, it is more likely that his/her doctrinal position will agree with yours. However, don't reject a counselor from another denomination over minor doctrinal conflicts. It is possible for two Christians to disagree on points of doctrine without affecting their ability to communicate. Be honest when you talk to him/her about how your beliefs differ. If you believe that the conflicts are too great, look for another counselor.

Be very sure to choose a counselor who has experience in dealing with victims of domestic violence. The information in this field is relatively new, and many counselors, highly qualified in other areas, are not aware of the issues involved. If the counselor does not know about the cycles of battering, or insinuates that you must be at fault if your husband has abused you, he is not capable of providing the help you need. Counseling with anyone who does not understand the reasons for battering, or its effects, could be worse than no counseling.

Your minister or other Christian counselor should have specific training in the counseling field. Sometimes a minister receives training at a seminary or Bible college, or takes post-graduate course work in counseling as a ministry. Christian counselors should be prepared to provide you with a list of their obligations during counseling. Carefully read their code of ethics, a list of your rights as their client, and their intent to provide designated counseling services for a specified fee.

Proper support comes from a counselor who displays an ability to help you determine some of your immediate and long-term needs. You should be satisfied with the ways the counselor approaches your problems, gives you information, and shows respect for your ability to choose what you will do. Most counselors are aware that they are helpers, not advisors; listeners, not lecturers. Your counselor must give you time to talk, think, pray, act and react. One who offers a "quick fix," or has all the answers for your problems may not understand your needs or may be attempting to manipulate you into making decisions without allowing you to determine what is best for you. A counselor may tell you honestly that he believes you are not taking enough responsibility for decision-making if you procrastinate. But if proper support is given, you will be able to make your own decisions based on what you know is right for you. Do not let someone else make your decisions for you.

Confidentiality is an important issue in counseling. If your counselor is your pastor or another church member, you have the right to expect that your situation will not be shared with his spouse, other church members, or your spouse. Ask the counselor frankly if he will maintain absolute confidentiality unless you sign a release of information form. This form would allow the counselor to share limited information about your situation with another person or agency for an express purpose specified on the form.

Many women have been humiliated or endangered because their counselor, for example, shared confidential information with his wife, who told her best friend, who told the Bible study class, etc. Because a church is like an extended family, it is easy for a person's confidentiality to be broken. Maintain your own confidentiality by refusing to discuss your situation with anyone who does not understand how important it is to remain silent.

The Secular Counselor

It is also possible that you can find a secular counselor with whom you can communicate, even if the counselor does not share your faith. It is very important that the secular counselor give full credence to the importance of the Word of God in your life. If he is not a Christian, it is vital that complete respect for your viewpoint, and how heavily it weighs in your decision-making, is given. Obviously, a counselor who gives you the feeling that Christianity is old-fashioned or not appropriate in light of the "science" of sociology or psychology will not be able to facilitate your need to reconcile your life with God's will.

Some secular counselors are Christians. Working in a secular agency does not preclude the possibility that your counselor has a strong personal faith in Christ. When you choose a counselor, explain that your beliefs govern your choices in your life, that they strengthen your resolve toward change, and that God's grace is your foundation and strength.

The secular counselor who is not a Christian may still be able to respect and admire your faith. It is possible for non-Christians to give you the support and information that you need emotionally and mentally. Feel free to express your faith with your counselor, and give him a chance to support you as much as possible. If you find that you need spiritual help, perhaps you can combine secular counseling and the help of a friend or other church member whose Christian walk is strong. Make sure that the Christian helper can give you support, confidentiality, help in Bible study, and serve as a prayer partner. Let your secular counselor know that you have called on your Christian helper to help you balance your support both emotionally and spiritually. If you become concerned about something your counselor says which seems unscriptural, ask your Christian helper to help you search God's Word for the answer. Take your reasons for disagreement back to your secular counselor, along with any alternatives you discover which would comply with Scripture. The secular counselor can help you explore these alternatives with an eye to your desire to be safe, adequate in your self-esteem, and in harmony with what you believe to be God's will.

The secular counselor, also, should be experienced in working with victims and batterers. Again, seek a counselor who does not display an attitude that you are to blame for the abuse in your home. Find a person knowledgeable about the causes and effects of violent relationships. If you think that the counselor sees you as a "neurotic" woman who needs counseling to help with issues other than those foremost in your mind, choose another counselor.

Secular counselors should provide you with a list of their obligations to you during counseling also. Many guarantee absolute confidentiality within their agency or office. You may sign information releases to Welfare, Children's Services, your lawyer or pastor, if you choose. Often, these releases state specifically the information which can be released in order for others to provide appropriate services for you. Ask your counselor what your husband would be told if he were to contact the counselor. You must feel free to discuss whatever concerns you may have without fearing they will be inappropriately shared.

What Do I Expect From Counseling?

Again, a worksheet format may help you decide what you think counseling can or should do for you. Make a list that includes your need for support, information, personal growth or spiritual help.

1) Describe what support system you already have: friends, family, pastor, doctor, etc.

155

2) What do you like best about discussing your situation with each person? What problems do you have in discussing with each? This will help you to explore what types of support you have found to be most helpful.

3) How will you find a competent counselor? (Ask your minister for a referral; call a Christian counseling center; look in the phone book under counseling or under Christian Outreach Centers; write or call the counseling centers listed in the back of this book, etc.)

4) Once you find some counselors, what questions will you ask in order to determine whether they are knowledgeable about domestic violence and its effects? Perhaps you could phrase your questions and concerns in this manner: "I am currently living with (or separated from) a man who has used physically, (and/or emotionally, spiritually) abusive behavior. Could you please tell me...."

a) What are your professional qualifications? (Licensed or certified as a counselor or mental health professional, trained para-professional, degrees in sociology or psychology, ordained minister with specific training for a counseling ministry.)

b) What experience do you have in working with victims of domestic violence and/or batterers?

c) What information can you provide about the cycle of violence, about the causes of domestic violence, and about some of my alternatives to living with the abuse?

d) What are the charges for your services?

e) Do you offer client services other than counseling? (Support groups, client advocacy at court or police station, shelter services, counseling for children, referrals to other agencies, help with parenting skills, etc.)

f) What statement will you provide me about my rights as a client? (Confidentiality, protection of client records, explanation of any testing procedures which may be used, statement of counselor's legal and ethical responsibilities.)

g) If this is a Christian counselor or agency: Is your counseling service inter-denominational, or do you accept only clients who adhere to your particular doctrines?

h) If this is a secular counselor or agency: Can you provide supportive and respectful counseling for a person with strong religious beliefs?

5) When you choose a counselor, what individual qualities would be most important to you? (Warm and friendly attitude or professionally detached attitude; woman or man; younger than you or older than you; Christian or non-Christian, etc.)

6) If you decide to seek counseling, what can you afford to pay, if anything?

7) With what area(s) do you need the most help? (Information, spiritual values, feelings, decision-making, self-esteem, proper assertiveness, etc.)

8) How many times per week would you like to see a counselor?

9) What availability would you expect? Do you need a counselor who can be reached by phone almost any time of the day or night, or can you work with one who sees you only at appointed times?

10) Do you expect the counselor to provide both emotional and spiritual support? How important is it for the counselor to share your religious convictions?

11) If you counsel with a non-Christian, list the Christian people with whom you would share your spiritual concerns, and to whom you would turn for help.

Another worksheet might list what you think are your responsibilities in counseling. Use this worksheet to reaffirm your ability to help yourself. Check to see that you are being realistic about what you or your counselor can accomplish.

What Are Your Responsibilities In Counseling?

1) Are you prepared to:
_____ be on time for appointments?
_____ inquire as to the fees for any services, and to pay the amount at the time agreed upon?
_____ complete any reading or lists that the counselor may ask you to do?
_____ be willing to attend counseling for a minimum specified period of time?
_____ consider submitting to standard psychological tests which have been explained to you, and expect to meet with your counselor to discuss the interpretation of the results?
_____ be willing to ask questions, to share specific incidents from your life, to explore your personal responsibilities to your husband and children?

2) What are your responsibilities if the counselor wants you to explore areas which are painful for you to discuss? Can you be honest with another person concerning your feelings or situation?

3) Do you feel free to accept or reject something your counselor says after you have thought and prayed about it, and to tell the counselor honestly what you think about his position on the matter?

4) Will you work with the counselor to develop new ways of accepting yourself, trying to apply to your life the information given to you, and learning to communicate your thoughts and feelings in an understandable and acceptable manner? What new behavior patterns do you need to learn?

5) What restrictions or suggestions will you accept from the counselor, even if they are difficult for you? (For example, some domestic violence counselors ask that you call them before attempting to contact your spouse if you and he are separated. They know how vulnerable you may be to his manipulations and want the opportunity to help you resist returning too soon, before he has changed his behavior.)

Chapter 12
The Narrow Path

"Thy word is a lamp unto my feet, and a light unto my path . . . . I am afflicted very much: quicken me, O Lord, according unto thy word." (Psalm 119:105,107)

Your Support Network

Take time right now to consider the blessings of friends, family, and other church members as supporters in your struggle. It is important. They can provide an atmosphere of safety and encourage your growth. This is an opportunity for you to take a careful look at what God intended when He lovingly placed these people in your life.

You may have been able to make new friends and become closer to your family recently during your growth from victimization to freedom. Whether relationships are newly made, friends you have maintained over the years, or ones reinstituted after a difficult time, they are some of God's greatest gifts in your life. As you move onto the narrow path which leads to God's fulfillment of your life, these relationships form a network of bonds woven with the threads of compassion, empathy, and sharing.

As you become more responsible in caring for yourself, you become better able to reach out to others. Part of this outreach is a growth toward self-judgment and the ability to help others through the pain you have endured. It is part of God's plan that adversity in our lives always seems to lead us to a richer understanding of someone else's burdens. Use the full knowledge of how God has so greatly eased you from darkness into light to offer hope to someone else who needs encouragement.

" . . . Whatsoever things are true, whatsoever things are honest, whatsoever things are just, whatsoever things are pure, whatsoever things are lovely, whatsoever things are of good report; if there be any virtue, and if there be any praise, think on these things. Those things, which ye have both learned, and received, and heard . . . do: and the God of peace shall be with you" (Philippians 4:8,9).

Part of maintaining relationships with friends, family, children, and spouse is knowing your own limits and recognizing someone else's boundaries. While your wounds heal, try not to lean too heavily on any one person. If you have a tendency to form addictive attachments to people, determine not to cling to anyone except God. Develop a multitude of friendships which allow you to share different viewpoints and activities.

Each friend or family member must also deal with his or her own issues. This necessarily limits the amount of energy they can expend helping you. The relationship could be damaged if you cannot accept this limited help. It is a mistake to think that only one person can understand or empathize with you. Respect however much time and help the person can freely give. Avoid repeating your story over and over. And try to give as much attention and affection as you take.

We often seem to believe that one friend or relative can provide every type of support we need. Look closely at your relationships. Be more aware and thankful that each offers a few specific ways in which it is unique. Your spouse may enjoy many of the activities you do together, but not share your love of music. Join a choir or begin to go to concerts with a friend who does. Do you have a friend with whom you can always laugh and who brightens your heart? Be thankful for her humor and do not try to force her to give more than she is able. Perhaps you have a friend whose intellectual interests closely match your own. Pursue those interests with her and avoid asking for an unreasonable depth of emotional support. Go to someone who uplifts you spiritually, who encourages you to study and listen to God's Word. If she does not share your interest in sports, be grateful that she fills your heart with peace. Each person whom God has arranged to interact with you has a special place in your life. Know your own needs, and give on whatever individual level you can to these special people.

It is important to reach outside yourself. Be concerned about co-workers, people in your church whom you barely know, and neighbors. If you find someone to be irritating, try to see beneath the surface to whatever pain may be causing it. The gossiper in the study group may be very insecure, thinking herself unable to hold anyone's attention unless she tells stories about others. If you look for the pain, it becomes easier to leave judgment to God. You do not need to condone her actions, nor should you allow yourself to be her victim. Try to show her that you are willing to listen to her if she can avoid gossip. Do not act self-righteous or condemn her. Simply reach for the person beneath the pain.

Standing Fast

Your own spiritual realignment is a lifelong process. With God's help, each hardship and joy will provide infinite opportunities for you to grow. Patience, compassion, and empathy develop slowly as they begin to replace bitterness and confusion. Change may be frightening, but it can be exciting and productive as well.

Ecclesiastes 3:1-8,11 speaks of life's changes, sufferings, and uncertainties—and God's ability to use them all in His glorious plan.

"To every thing there is a season, and a time to every purpose under the heaven:

"A time to be born, and a time to die; a time to plant, and a time to pluck up that which is planted;

"A time to kill, and a time to heal; a time to break down, and a time to build up;

163

"A time to weep, and a time to laugh; a time to mourn, and a time to dance;

"A time to cast away stones, and a time to gather stones together; a time to embrace, and a time to refrain from embracing;

"A time to get, and a time to lose; a time to keep, and time to cast away;

"A time to rend, and a time to sew; a time to keep silence, and a time to speak;

"A time to love and a time to hate; a time of war, and a time of peace.

" . . . He hath made every thing beautiful in his time: also he hath set the world in their heart, so that no man can find out the work that God maketh from the beginning to the end."

You have God's promise: "And God is able to make all grace abound toward you; that ye, always having all sufficiency in all things, may abound to every good work" (II Corinthians 9:8). He has given you valuable tools with which to construct a loving, godly woman who will live as God commands. These tools are specific in their function, and all of them serve to keep each part of you functioning well. Self-esteem, reconciliation with the past, knowledge of your own strengths and weaknesses and dependence upon God's unconditional love will enable you to stand fast as the woman God intends you to be.

Jesus lived and died and rose again in order for you to be free from the bondage of sin. As you grow in God's Word, may you find peace in His perfect will.

"I will not leave you comfortless: I will come to you . . . .
"Let not your heart be troubled, neither let it be afraid . . . .
"Arise, let us go hence."   (John 14:18,27,31)

A Special Note to the Reader

Perhaps you are feeling very unloved right now—maybe even unlovable. Perhaps you do not know what it means to have a personal, loving relationship with Jesus Christ.

If that is so, perhaps you would like to accept Christ as your Saviour. You can.

Jesus is the holy, perfect Son of God. Almost 2,000 years ago, in fulfillment of the Father's plan, He came to earth. Was born as the infant son of a virgin named Mary. Grew to manhood, and preached for three years so that all would know why He came. "I have come as light into the world, that everyone who believes in Me may not remain in darkness . . . . I did not come to judge the world, but to save the world" (John 12:46,47).

Christ assumed the burden of our sins. He willingly accepted the death penalty that was ours, so that we might accept His atonement and escape the penalty of sin. Romans 6:23 tells us that " . . . the wages of sin is death; but the free gift of God is eternal life in Jesus Christ our Lord."

Yes, we are all sinners. Romans 3:23 says, "for all have sinned and fall short of the glory of God." We all deserve the penalty of death. But because God loves us, He sent His Son to die in our place. "But God demonstrates His own love toward us, in that while we were yet sinners, Christ died for us" (Romans 5:8).

But that isn't all He did. If all He did was die, our hope of eternal life and of life worth living now would be empty, useless. No. More than that, after three days in the grave following His crucifixion, Christ rose—triumphant eternally over death and sin. " . . . Christ died for our sins according to the Scriptures, and that He was buried, and that He was raised on the third day according to the Scriptures, and that He

165

appeared to Cephas, then to the twelve. After that, He appeared to more than five hundred brethren at one time . . . " (I Corinthians 15:3-6). And in that we have victory! "O death, where is your victory? O death, where is your sting? The sting of death is sin, and the power of sin is the law; but thanks be to God, who gives us the victory through our Lord Jesus Christ" (I Corinthians 15:55-57).

That victory can be yours, right now if you want it. First, you must believe that you are a sinner, that you have done things which a perfectly holy God cannot accept. If you died right now, you would be lost forever. (See Hebrews 9:27.)

Then, you must believe that Jesus Christ is God's Son and that through His death and resurrection, the penalty has been paid for your sins. John 3:16 says, "For God so loved the world, that He gave His only begotten Son, that whoever believes in Him should not perish, but have eternal life."

That whoever means you. You can put your own name in place of the word. See also I Peter 1:18,19.

You can claim this love and forgiveness for yourself. To do so, you must call upon Christ in faith, believing that He is who He says He is, and confess Him as Lord and Saviour.

Romans 10:9,10, and 13 tell us that, " . . . if you confess with your mouth Jesus as Lord, and believe in your heart that God raised Him from the dead, you shall be saved; for with the heart man believes, resulting in righteousness, and with the mouth he confesses, resulting in salvation . . . . for whoever will call upon the name of the Lord will be saved."

Would you like to do that right now? It is our hope and prayer that if you do not already know Christ as Saviour, that you will acknowledge your sin, ask Christ to forgive you, and believe in Him. It doesn't mean the problems will miraculously vanish. But it does mean rest and peace in the midst of the trouble. "Peace I leave with you; My peace I give to you; not as the world gives, do I give to you. Let not your heart be troubled, nor let it be fearful" (John 14:27).

(All Scripture quoted from New American Standard Bible.)

Resources

Resources

The following list of resources and counselors should not be construed as an endorsement by the publisher or the author. There are numerous highly qualified counseling centers and counselors available throughout the country. These suggestions are given as a starting point to find the comfort and professional guidance sometimes necessary during times of intense emotional turmoil.

The following lists have been compiled to aid battered women and violent men find appropriate counseling. Both Christian and secular counseling facilities have been listed. I wish to thank the National Association of Nouthetic Counselors and the National Coalition Against Domestic Violence for providing the listings.

Domestic violence victims can look in the phone book under "Churches" for local Christian Outreach Centers which provide counseling. A local minister or the Salvation Army may be able to refer a battered woman or her husband to a Christian counselor. These counseling centers can provide additional information.

Each state now has secular organizations which deal with domestic violence. Women may look under "Domestic Violence" or "Women's Centers" in the phone book, or may write or call her state coalition to find the nearest center. More information can be obtained from:

The National Coalition Against Domestic Violence
2401 Virginia Avenue, N.W., Suite 305
Washington, D.C. 20037
(202) 293-8860

Some state coalitions also provide batterer's programs or services. For Christian counseling, men may contact the Christian counseling center(s) in their states. A complete list of secular batterer's services nationwide is published by RAVEN in the National Directory of Programs for Men. The cost at this printing is $8.00 plus $2.00 postage and handling. To order the directory you may write:

EMV (Ending Men's Violence) Directory
c/o RAVEN
P.O. Box 24159
St. Louis, MO 63130

BIBLICAL COUNSELING COORDINATORS/USA

ALASKA

Rev. Byron Green
Abbot Loop Christian Ctr.
2626 Abbot Road
Anchorage, AK 99507
(907) 349-9641

ARKANSAS

Citadel Bible College
Attn: Dr. Paul Brombach
Ozark, AR 72449

Harold Hill
THE LIFE HOUSE
P.O. Box 1236
Little Rock, AR 72203
(501) 372-3678

Curtis Thomas
Bible Ch. of Little Rock
8115 Ascension Road
Little Rock, AR 72204
(501) 562-0792

ARIZONA

Rev. Jim Adams
4248 E. Broadway
Mesa, AZ 85206
(602) 830-4829 - home
(602) 832-1150

CALIFORNIA

Rev. John Cully
Evangelical Book Store
3752 - 30th St.
San Diego, CA 92104
(619) 291-4381

CALIFORNIA (con't.)

Rev. Jim Eller
Grace Baptist Church
8223 California
Riverside, CA 92504
(714) 359-1593 - home
(714) 688-3460

Rev. Carl E. Erickson
356 Arroyo Drive
So. San Francisco, CA 94080
(415) 871-7107 - home
(415) 583-9020 - church

Rev. Jay Fluck
Calvary Pres. Church
12120 La Mirada Blvd.
La Mirada, CA 90638
(213) 943-2671 - church
(213) 929-2150 - home

Rev. George Scipione
2620 Keen Drive
San Diego, CA 92139
(619) 475-4635

Rev. Robert Sommerville
Evangelical Free Church
1819 E. Seeger Ave.
Visalia, CA 93277
(209) 627-3912

DELAWARE

Rev. Charles Betters
Red Lion Evangelical Assn.
Box 176
Bear, DE 19701
(302) 834-8588

FLORIDA

James & Mary Ann Ade
4831 Malpas Lane
Jacksonville, FL 32210
(904) 389-1822

Rev. Jeff K. Boer
Sharon Orthodox Pres. Ch.
675 W. 68th St.
Hialeah, FL 33114
(305) 821-0693

Rev. Bob Bole
8487 Boysenberry Lane
Jacksonville, FL 32244
(904) 778-1039

Mr. & Mrs. William Cox
5751 NE 20th Terrace
Ft. Lauderdale, FL 33308
(305) 491-1742

Dr. Howard Eyrich
Granada Pres. Church
950 University Drive
Coral Gables, FL 33134
(305) 667-4850
(305) 444-4622 - office

Rev. Neil Gilmour
17920 S.W. 88th Ct.
Miami, FL 33157
(305) 255-8146

Dr. Lonie Snelling
Royal Palm Bib. Cnslng. Ctr.
7224 Colonial Blvd., S.E.
Ft. Myers, FL 33908
(813) 275-6651

GEORGIA

J. Todd Adams
4586 Roswell Rd., Apt. C-1
Atlanta, GA 30342
(404) 843-0111

Rev. Chuck Frost
Dayspring Pres. Church
425 Pecan Circle
Forsyth, GA 31029
(912) 994-4261

Dr. John Grauley
682 Mulberry St.
Macon, GA 31201
(912) 746-3223

Dr. Harry McGee
311 E. Hall St.
Savannah, GA 31499
(912) 236-9506

Dr. E. Franklin Payne
First Pres. Church
303 Kennelworth Place
Augusta, GA 30909
(404) 828-4576
(404) 736-1506

HAWAII

Rev. Peter Anderson
Trinity Pres. Church
P.O. Box 876
Kailua, HI 96734

ILLINOIS

Rev. David Cummings
6931 Highland
Hanover Park, IL 60103
(312) 289-9031 - home
(312) 365-4747 - church

Rev. Vince Leach
Keeneyville Bible Church
6 N 171 Gary Ave.
Roselle, IL 60172
(312) 830-1251 - home
(312) 529-8949 - office

Rev. Robert Sheridan
Palos Bible Church
12701 S. 70th Ave.
Palos Heights, IL 60463
(312) 361-5479 - home
(312) 448-2223

Rev. Tom Walker
1013 S. Highland
Oak Park, IL 60304
(312) 386-2747 - home
(312) 749-2688 - office

Rev. Wes Walters
117 N. Hamilton St.
Marissa, IL 62257
(618) 295-2063

INDIANA

Rev. Bruce Bigelow
Lake Hills Baptist Ch.
9209 W. 85th Ave.
Schererville, IN 46375
(219) 365-5682 - home
(219) 365-4747 - church

INDIANA (con't.)

Rev. William Goode
Faith Baptist Church
1441 Warren Place
Lafayette, IN 47905
(317) 474-5332

Dr. Robert Smith
5401 E. 200 N
Lafayette, IN 47905
(317) 589-8565

Rev. Robert Yawberg
1638 Spring St.
Fort Wayne, IN 46808

KANSAS

Jim Morris
714 N. West St., Ste. B
Wichita, KS 67203
(316) 942-5572 - office
(316) 733-0104

Rev. Don Scott
Union Center Bldg.
150 N. Main St., Ste. 926
Wichita, KS 67202
(316) 263-5869 - office
(316) 684-1703

LOUISIANA

Rev. Dana Stoddard
416 N. Pine St.
DeRidder, LA 70634
(318) 462-3911

MASSACHUSETTS

Rev. Lloyd Jonas
Forestdale Baptist Ch.
11 Tabor Rd., Box 522
Forestdale, MA 02644
(617) 477-1307

MARYLAND

Bill O'Rourke (M.D.)
150 W. Main St.
Westminster, MD 21157
(301) 848-3818 - office
(301) 848-2722

Rev. James Raun
7515 Harford Rd.
Baltimore, MD 21234
(301) 444-6233

MICHIGAN

Rev. Harold Ballew
Brotherhood Chris. Ch.
515 S. Lafayette
Royal Oak, MI 48067
(313) 548-6398

Grand Rapids Bapt. Sem.
Dr. A.L. Fortosis
1001 E. Beltline
Grand Rapids, MI 49505
(616) 949-5300

Mrs. Kay Wagner
36579 Quakertown Rd.
Farmington Hills, MI 48018
(313) 476-2720

MINNESOTA

Mr. Steven Coalwell
Box 55
Hackensack, MN 56452
(218) 675-6835

MISSOURI

Rev. Norman Hoeflinger
4206 N. Colorado Ave.
Kansas City, MO 64117
(816) 455-0384

MISSISSIPPI

Rev. Jim Baird
First Pres. Ch. of Amer.
Box 4862
Jackson, MS 39216
(601) 353-8316 - office
(601) 355-6315 - home

Rev. Walt Shepherd
Covenant Pres. Church
P.O. Box 4292
Laurel, MS 39441
(601) 425-4115

NEW MEXICO

Mr. Laury Eck
315 Arno
Albuquerque, NM 87103
(505) 243-6887

MONTANA

Rev. Al Edwards
18 Heather Rd.
Billings, MT 59105
(406) 248-5777

NEW YORK

Rev. John McConaughy
Alps Baptist Church
Box 285
West Sand Lake, NY 12196
(518) 674-5304

Chris Miller
Word of Life
Route 9
Schroon Lake, NY 12870
(518) 532-7111

Rev. William Whiteman
31 S. Broad St., Box 96
Morris, NY 13808
(607) 263-5147

OHIO

Rev. Howard Hart
4325 Hegner Ave.
Cincinnati, OH 45236
(513) 791-5254

Rev. Joseph Propri
1639 Lyntz Rd., S.W.
Lordstown, OH 44481
(216)824-2612

OREGON

Rev. Dwight Custis
Trinity Bible Church
Box 16732
Portland, OR 97216
(503) 255-0357

Rev. Don Poundstone
1st Orth. Pres. Ch. of Portland
624 N.E. 63 Ave.
Portland, OR 97213
(503) 233-7858

PENNSYLVANIA

Rev. Chuck Bridger
Ambassador Ministries, Inc.
1028 Anna Rd.
Huntingdon Valley, PA 19006
(215) 379-4687

Rev. Rick Horne
Faith Reformed Bapt. Ch.
44 Green Hill Rd.
Media, PA 19063
(215) 872-7600
(215) 565-0890

Rev. Lee Maliska
Chris. Cnslng. Ctr. of Bucks Co.
875 N. Easton Rd.
Doylestown, PA 18901
(215) 345-8707

Dr. Willard McMillan
Geneva College
1329 Book Ave.
Beaver Falls, PA 15010
(412) 846-5100, Ext. 238

Rev. Jack Schilthuis
Memorial Park Pres. Ch.
8800 Peebles Rd.
Allison Park, PA 15101
(412) 364-9492

Rev. Dean Smith
College Hill Ref. Pres. Ch.
3217 College Ave.
Beaver Falls, PA 15010
(412) 843-4840

SOUTH CAROLINA

Rev. Earl Eckerson
Mitchell Road Pres. Ch.
207 Mitchell Rd.
Greenville, SC 29615
(803) 268-2218

SOUTH DAKOTA

Mr. and Mrs. Peter Grossman
135 River Rd.
Pierre, SD 57501
(605) 224-1951

TENNESSEE

Mr. James Dixon
1031 Union St.
Shelbyville, TN 37160
(615) 684-0193

Rev. James Jones
Asbury Pres. Ch.
1065 Ingleside Terrace
Johnson City, TN 37601
(615) 926-8921

Dr. Joe Neumann
207 West G Street
Elizabethton, TN 37643
(615) 543-4640

TEXAS

Rev. Jack Berg
Sun Valley Bapt. Temple
9901 McCombs
El Paso, TX 79924
(915) 755-7232 - office
(915) 755-1155

TEXAS (con't.)

Mrs. Ruth Booker
2209 Emerson Lane
Denton, TX 76201
(817) 387-1476

Rev. Kent Hinkson
16319 Fox Crossing Ln.
Spring, TX 77379
(713) 376-3441

John Morris
Grace Community Church
3215 Jacksonville Rd.
Tyler, TX 75701
(214) 593-3800

VIRGINIA

Rev. Phil Graham
101 Berrington Ct.
Richmond, VA 23221
(804) 358-1283

Dr. Ron Hawkins
Liberty Baptist College
Lynchburg, VA 24506
(804) 237-5961

Mr. Robert Schneider
Biblical Cnslng. Foundation
5540 Colfax Ave.
Alexandria, VA 22311
(703) 931-4164

WASHINGTON

Rev. Mark McKay
SW Seattle Chris. Ctr.
10300 - 28th Ave., SW
Seattle, WA 98146
(206) 932-0186

WYOMING

Rev. Craig Rowe
8209 Powderhouse Rd.
Cheyenne, WY 82009
(307) 638-8201

BIBLICAL COUNSELING COORDINATORS/International

CANADA

Dr. Richard Ganz
135 Pleasant Park Rd.
Ottawa, Ont. K1H 5M4
(613) 731-1752

* This list provided by Christian Counseling Institute of Lancaster.
Reprinted by permission.

STATE DOMESTIC VIOLENCE COALITIONS

ALABAMA

Alabama Coalition Against
  Domestic Violence
P.O. Box 4762
Montgomery, AL 36101
(205) 263-0677

ALASKA

Alaska Network on Domestic
  Violence and Sexual Assault
130 Seward Street #501
Juneau, AK 99801

ARIZONA

Arizona Coalition Against
  Domestic Violence
c/o Barbara Damon
P.O. Box 42378
Tucson, AZ 85733
(602) 792-0285

ARKANSAS

Arkansas Coalition Against Violence to Women and Children
433 Hall Building
209 West Capitol
Little Rock, AR 72201
(501) 375-2225
1-800-332-4443

CALIFORNIA (Central)

Central California Coalition
  Against Domestic Violence
P.O. Box 3931
Modesto, CA 95352
(209) 575-7037

CALIFORNIA (Southern)

So. California Coalition on
  Battered Women
P.O. Box 5036
Santa Monica, CA 90405
(213) 392-9874

CALIFORNIA (Northern)

No. California Shelter Support
  Service
930 North Commerce
Stockton, CA 95202

COLORADO

Colorado Domestic Violence
  Coalition
P.O. Box 18902
Denver, CO 80218
(303) 894-2810

CONNECTICUT

Connecticut Coalition Against
  Domestic Violence
Attn: Anne Meare
22 Maple Avenue
Hartford, CT 06114
(203) 524-5890

DELAWARE

Delaware Commission for
  Women
Department of Community Affairs
Carvel State Building
820 North French Street
Wilmington, DE 19801
(302) 571-2660

DISTRICT OF COLUMBIA

D.C. Coalition Against Domestic
Violence
c/o WLDF
2000 P Street, NW, Suite 400
Washington, D.C. 20036

FLORIDA

Refuge Information Network of
Florida
P.O. Box 6041-E
Orlando, FL 32853
(305) 886-2856

GEORGIA

Georgia Network Against
Domestic Violence
250 Georgia Avenue, SE
Suite 367
Atlanta, GA 30312
(404) 524-3847

HAWAII

Hawaii State Committee on
Family Violence
1100 Alakea Street, Room 429
Honolulu, HI 96813
(808) 538-7216

IDAHO

Idaho Council on Domestic
Violence
P.O. Box 55
Boise, ID 83607
(208) 334-4171

ILLINOIS

Illinois Coalition Against
Domestic Violence
937 South Fourth Street
Springfield, IL 62703
(217)789-2830
State Hotline #: (800) 334-SAFE

INDIANA

Indiana Coalition Against
Domestic Violence
104½ E. Kirkwood Ave., #9
Bloomington, IN 47401
Toll Free: (800) 334-SAFE

IOWA

Iowa Coalition Against
Domestic Violence
c/o Dianne Fagner
Family Violence Center
1101 Walnut
Des Moines, IA 50309
(515) 243-6147

KANSAS

Kansas Association of Domestic
Violence Programs
Box 1883
Topeka, KS 66601
(913) 841-6887

KENTUCKY

Kentucky Domestic Violence
Association
c/o Women's Crisis Center
321 York Street
Newport, KY 41701
(606) 581-6282

178

Resources

LOUISIANA

Louisiana Coalition Against
  Domestic Violence
c/o Capital Area Family Violence
  Intervention Center
P.O. Box 2133
Baton Rouge, LA 70821
(504) 389-3001

MAINE

Maine Coalition for Family Crisis
  Services
P.O. Box 642
Rockland, ME 04841
(207) 594-2128

MARYLAND

Maryland Network Against
  Domestic Violence
c/o Ruth Edwards (1986-87)
CASA
Gorman Plaza, Suite 124
8950 Route 108
Columbia, MD 21045
(301) 997-CASA

MASSACHUSETTS

Massachusetts Coalition of
  Battered Women's Service
  Groups
20 East Street
Boston, MA 02111
(617) 426-8492

MICHIGAN

Michigan Coalition Against
  Domestic Violence
10435 Lincoln
Huntington Woods, MI 48070
(313) 961-0290

MINNESOTA

Minnesota Coalition for
  Battered Women
435 Aldine Street
St. Paul, MN 55104
(612) 646-6177

MISSISSIPPI

Mississippi Coalition Against
  Domestic Violence
P.O. Box 333
Biloxi, MS 39533
(601) 436-3809

MISSOURI

Missouri Coalition Against
  Domestic Violence
2838 Olive
St. Louis, MO 63103
(314) 531-9101

MONTANA

Montana Coalition Against
  Domestic Violence
c/o Battered Women's Network
P.O. Box 752
Bozeman, MT 59715
(406) 586-0263

NEBRASKA

Nebraska Task Force on
  Domestic Violence and Sexual
  Assault
YWCA
222 South 29th Street
Omaha, NE 68131
(402) 345-6555

179

NEVADA

Nevada Network Against
Domestic Violence
625 Fairview, Suite 116
Carson City, NV 89701
(702) 882-6209
State Hotline #: (800) 992-5757

NEW HAMPSHIRE

New Hampshire Coalition
Against Domestic and Sexual
Violence
P.O. Box 353
Concord, NH 03301
(603) 224-8893
State Hotline #: (800) 852-3311
(Multi-Issue Hotline)

NEW JERSEY

New Jersey Coalition for
Battered Women
206 West State Street
Trenton, NJ 08608
State Hotline #: (800) 572-7233
(609) 695-1758

NEW MEXICO

New Mexico State Coalition
Against Domestic Violence
P.O. Box 2463
Las Cruces, NM 88004
(505) 526-2819

NEW YORK

New York State Coalition Against
Domestic Violence
5 Neher Street
Woodstock, NY 12498
(914) 679-5231
State Hotline: (800) 942-6906
—Eng.
State Hotline: (800) 942-6908
—Span.

NORTH CAROLINA

North Carolina Coalition Against
Domestic Violence
P.O. Box 877
Concord, NC 28026-0877
(704) 786-9317

NORTH DAKOTA

North Dakota Council on Abused
Women's Services
State Networking Office
418 E. Rosser Ave., Ste. 210
Bismarck, ND 58501
(702) 255-6240
State Hotline #: (800) 472-2911

OHIO

Action Ohio Coalition for
Battered Women
P.O. Box 15673
Columbus, OH 43215
(614) 221-1255

OKLAHOMA

Oklahoma Coalition on Domestic
Violence and Sexual Assault
c/o YWCA
129 NW 5th
Oklahoma City, OK 73102
(405) 232-7681
State Hotline #: (800) 522-SAFE

OREGON

Oregon Coalition Against
Domestic Violence and Sexual
Assault
2336 SE Belmont Street
Portland, OR 97214
(503) 239-4486/4487

PENNSYLVANIA

Pennsylvania Coalition Against
Domestic Violence
2250 Elmerton Avenue
Harrisburg, PA 17110
(717) 652-9671

RHODE ISLAND

Rhode Island Council on
Domestic Violence
324 Broad Street
Central Falls, RI 02863
(401) 723-3051

SOUTH CAROLINA

South Carolina Coalition Against
Domestic Violence and Sexual
Assault
P.O. Box 7291
Columbia, SC 29202
(803) 799-0766

SOUTH DAKOTA

South Dakota Coalition Against
Domestic Violence and Sexual
Assault
c/o Children's Inn
615 South Grange
Sioux Falls, SD 57104
(605) 338-4880

TENNESSEE

Tennessee Task Force on Family
Violence
P.O. Box 120972
Nashville, TN 37212-0972
(615) 242-8288

TEXAS

Texas Council on Family Violence
1704 West 6th, Suite 200
Austin, TX 78703
(512) 482-8200
State Hotline #: (800) 223-8017

UTAH

Utah Domestic Violence Council
c/o Division of Family Services
150 West North Temple
Salt Lake City, UT 84103
(801) 355-2846

VERMONT

Vermont Domestic Violence
Programs
c/o Cindy Watson
UMBRELLA, INC.
One Prospect Avenue
St. Johnsbury, VT 05819
(802) 748-8645

VIRGINIA

Virginians Against Domestic
    Violence
P.O. Box 5692
Richmond, VA 23220
(804) 780-3505

WASHINGTON

Washington State Shelter
    Network
P.O. Box 677
110 E. 5th, Room 214
Olympia, WA 98507
(206) 753-4621
State Hotline: (800) 562-6025

WEST VIRGINIA

YWCA of Wheeling, West Virginia
    Coalition Against Domestic
    Violence, Family Refuge
    Service
1100 Chapline Street
Wheeling, WV 26003
(304) 645-6334

WISCONSIN

Wisconsin Coalition Against
    Domestic Violence
1051 Williamson Street
Madison, WI 53703
(608) 255-0539

WYOMING

Wyoming Coalition Against
    Domestic Violence and Sexual
    Assault
P.O. Box 1621
Cheyenne, WY 82003
(307) 754-7192

* This list provided by the National Coalition Against Domestic
Violence. Reprinted by permission.

Bibliography

Bibliography

Ankeny, Margaret E., Ed., Family Violence: A Cycle Of Abuse. Laramie, Wyoming, Center For Research, Service and Publication, University of Wyoming, 1979

Armstrong, Louise, *The Home Front: Notes From the Family War Zone.* New York, N.Y.: McGraw-Hill Book Company, 1983

Bridges, Jerry, *The Practice of Godliness,* Colorado Springs, Colorado: NavPress, 1986

Butler, Sandra, *Conspiracy Of Silence.* San Francisco: New Glide Publications, 1978

Boyer, Patricia A., and Jeffrey, Ronnald J., *A Guide For The Family Therapist.* New York, N.Y.: Jason Aronson, Inc. 1984

Brand, Paul, M.D. and Yancy, Philip, *Fearfully and Wonderfully Made.* Grand Rapids, Michigan: Zondervan Publishing House, 1980

Brownmiller, Susan, *Against Our Will.* New York, N.Y.: Simon and Schuster, Inc., 1975

Burgess, A.W.: Groth, A.N.: Holmstrom, L.L.: & Sgroi, S.M., *Sexual Assault of Children and Adolescents.* Lexington: Lexington Books, 1978

Carlson, Dwight, L., M.D., *Guilt Free.* Eugene, Oregon: Harvest House Publishers, 1983

Carlson, Dwight L., M.D., *Overcoming Hurts and Anger,* Eugene Oregon: Harvest House Publishers, 1981

Chapman, Jane R., and Gates, Margaret, *The Victimization Of Women.* Beverly Hills, California: Sage Publications, 1978

Charles, Sylvia, *Women In The Word.* South Plainfield, New Jersey: Bridge Publishing, 1984

Davidson, Terry, *Conjugal Crime: Understanding And Changing The Wife-Beating Pattern.* New York, N.Y.: Hawthorn Books, 1978

Dobson, James, Ph.D., *Dr. Dobson Answers Your Questions.* Wheaton, Illinois: Tyndale House Publishers, Inc., 1982

Dobson, James, Ph.D., *Emotions, Can You Trust Them?* Ventura, California: Regal Books, 1980

Dobson, James, Ph.D., *Love Must Be Tough.* Waco, Texas: Word Books, 1983

Donaldson, Margaret, *Children's Minds.* New York, N.Y.: Norton and Co., Inc., 1978

Elliot, Elisabeth, *A Lamp For My Feet.* Ann Arbor, Mich.: Vine Books, Servant Publications, 1985

Federal Bureau of Investigation: Uniform Crime Reports for the United States. Washington, D.C.: U.S. Department of Justice, 1978-82

Fleming, Jennifer Baker, *Stopping Wife Abuse.* Garden City, New York: Anchor Books, Anchor Press/Doubleday, 1979

Fugate, Richard J., *What The Bible Says About . . . Child Training.* Tempe, Arizona: Aletheia Publishers, Inc. 1980

Gattozzi, Ruth, Ph.D., *What's Wrong With My Child?* New York, N.Y.: McGraw-Hill Book Co., 1986

Gil, Eliana, *Outgrowing The Pain: A Book For and About Adults Abused As Children.* San Francisco: Launch Press, 1983

Goldstein, Jeffrey H., *Aggression And Crimes of Violence,* New York, N.Y.: Oxford University Press, 1975

Greenspan, Miriam, *A New Approach To Women and Therapy.* New York: McGraw-Hill, 1983

Hofeller, Kathleen, *Battered Women, Shattered Lives.* Saratoga, CA: R & E Publishers, 1980